How to Draw People

Learn How to Draw Portraits and Human Figures

By Robert Nortman

Table of Contents

Disclaimer

While all attempts have been made to verify the information provided in this book, the author does assume any responsibility for errors, omissions, or contrary interpretations of the subject matter contained within. The information provided in this book is for educational and entertainment purposes only. The reader is responsible for his or her own actions and the author does not accept any responsibilities for any liabilities or damages, real or perceived, resulting from the use of this information.

The trademarks that are used are without any consent, and the publication of the trademark is without permission or backing by the trademark owner. All trademarks and brands within this book are for clarifying purposes only and are the owned by the owners themselves, not affiliated with this document.

Introduction

Since you have picked up **How to draw People- Learn How to Draw Women's and Men's Portraits, Human Figures;** it obviously means that you have decided to draw beautiful human portraits and complete figures. But, it takes much more than just talent to draw accurate human figures. If you are an artist, we are sure that you are a master of drawing and sketching. However, when it comes to drawing a portrait, and that too live portrait; most of the artists freeze.

In this book, you will find some tips and tricks to draw accurate human features and complete figures. Each illustration has been explained with step by step tutorials along with the required text in detail. You will not feel any dearth of explanation in this book.

In the first section of this book, you will find an explanation of why we are always scared of attempting portraits. In addition, you will also find some useful tips on drawing human faces using proportion. Section 2 deals with the illustrations along with the summary of steps.

Without any hesitation, pick a pencil and your tools for shading while you go ahead with this book. Read and study each chapter while practicing the illustrations. Just a couple of drawings will give you the confidence of drawing more human illustrations all by yourself.

Good luck!

Section 1
Chapter 1
Why is a Stigma Attached to Drawing Faces of People?

Most of the artists get Goosebumps when they are asked to draw the portrait of a human. It is not because they are not competent enough. It is just because they are afraid that the portrait might not exactly look like the human face they intend to draw. Thus, it is the quality of "likeliness" that makes the best of artists shy away from drawing human figures.

On the contrary, when someone is asked to draw a generic human figure, which does not resemble anybody on Earth, they can happily grab a pencil and sit down to draw.

Why is resemblance in faces so hard to attain?

It is not at all difficult to attain likeliness or resemblance to a human face. It is just our own "logical" brain, which thinks in a particular manner and stops us from drawing accurately. The symbol or picture of lips that you carry in your head does not resemble the lips on the face that you want to draw. The same thing happens with all the features of the face. We tend to think in the "logical" way and think too much before we even sit to draw. You need to keep your symbols of the mind aside and draw what actually your eyes can see. If the nose of the person in front of you is a little twisted, draw a twisted nose. Do not think that it might not look right. When you finish drawing, it will definitely come out well.

What else you need to understand?

There are three concepts that you need to grasp if you intend to make a decent portrait:

- Perspective and proportion

- Drawing precise contours

- Giving accurate shading

Perspective and proportion: To get the perfect proportion, you need to have an accurate of system of measurement using your pencil. Trust your measurements and disregard the "logical' suggestions of your mind. Similarly, use the measurements to have a correct perspective of the face. If the face is a little turned on one side, the features will dramatically change in perspective and proportion.

Drawing precise contours: Contours are the outlines of the face and body, which must be drawn accurately to achieve the quality of likeliness. If you find the arms of a person a little longer than usual, let them be similar in your drawing. Similarly, if you see the *ponch* sticking out of the rim of the denims of a girl, just draw it. Do not try to perfect it.

Giving accurate shading: After you have achieved the perfect drawing, you need to give proper shading to the human figure you have drawn. Shading makes all the difference between a realistic and an unrealistic drawing. It must not be too dark or too light. Observe the source of light on the face and body and shade accordingly. You can use various tools to achieve accurate shading.

Chapter 2
How to Bring a Face to Life?

While achieving likeliness can be quite a challenge, faces and heads are some of the most difficult things to sketch. After you have taken the challenge of drawing accurate human faces and figures, you need to develop a habit of observing peoples' bodies from the perspective of an artist. Do not offend anyone, but ask for the permission of a person if you want to observe them closely. You can keep the following tips in mind if you want to draw perfect human faces.

Notice the proportions

Heads are not in the shape of perfect circles or ovals. You might think of them like the shape of an egg, whose end is a little tapered. Even this may vary with different people, especially men and your angle of vision.

The jaw line should be refined

The jaw line of women is much like the tapered end of an egg. But, it is a different case with men. They have a flatter chin and a more bony jaw.

The placement of eyes and gap between them

We normally think that the eyes are closer to the topmost edge of the head. But, their placement is totally different. They are almost halfway between the summit of the head and the base of the jaw. The space above the eyes is filled with our hairline. The gap between the eyes is equal to the width of the nose. You can also say that the eyes have a gap of almost one eye between them.

The width of the head

A basic rule for drawing a head is that the head is about the width of 5 eyes placed adjacent to each other. This rule applies only in case of drawing portraits. The proportions may vary in case of drawing complete human figures.

The placement of ears

The top edge of the ears is placed just above the location of eyes. Bring down the ears almost halfway between the eyes and the end of the jaw. The ears may have different shapes in different persons. Thus, you just need good observation while drawing ears.

The placement of nose and its shape

The nose ends almost where the ears end. Thus, you do not have to think much about the length of the nose. But, be careful about its width. You already know that there is a gap of almost one eye between the two eyes. And that is also equal to the width of the nose. But, while drawing the face of an elderly person, you might observe that the nose is a little thicker and wider than normal.

Draw the mouth carefully

Draw a very light guideline from the end of earlobes till the bottom of the jaw. The middle point of this guideline is the bottom of the lower lip. The corners of the lips extend till the placement of iris of the eyes.

Placement of the eyebrows

The width of the eyebrows is generally more than the eyes lying underneath. They are also thickest at the place where there is bridge of the nose. They taper while graduating outwards and sweep downwards as they end.

Do not place the hair on top of the head

The hair line starts from about one third to a quarter of the area between the eyebrows and top of the head. The hairs are not just placed on top of the head.

Chapter 3
Using Proportions in Different Cases

In Case of a Woman

The proportions mentioned above are just appropriate for a woman's face as well. The jaw line is a little more rounded in women; the ears are a little smaller, and the neck is a little narrower.

Using proportions in profile portraits

You can use all these proportions in for sketching heads in profiles too. Just extend these lines of proportion you used in the front view, to the face drawn in side view and you can keep your proportions consistent.

Section 2
Chapter 1
How to Draw Portrait of a Female Model?

Step 1

Let us start with drawing a portrait of a female model. Using the guidelines of proportions mentioned in Section 1, draw the basic outline of a female face. The girl we are drawing here has lifted her face slightly upwards. This has made a little difference in the shape of eyes. She is looking slightly downwards and her lips are slightly open. The hairs are covering both sides of her face and hence, the ears are not visible.

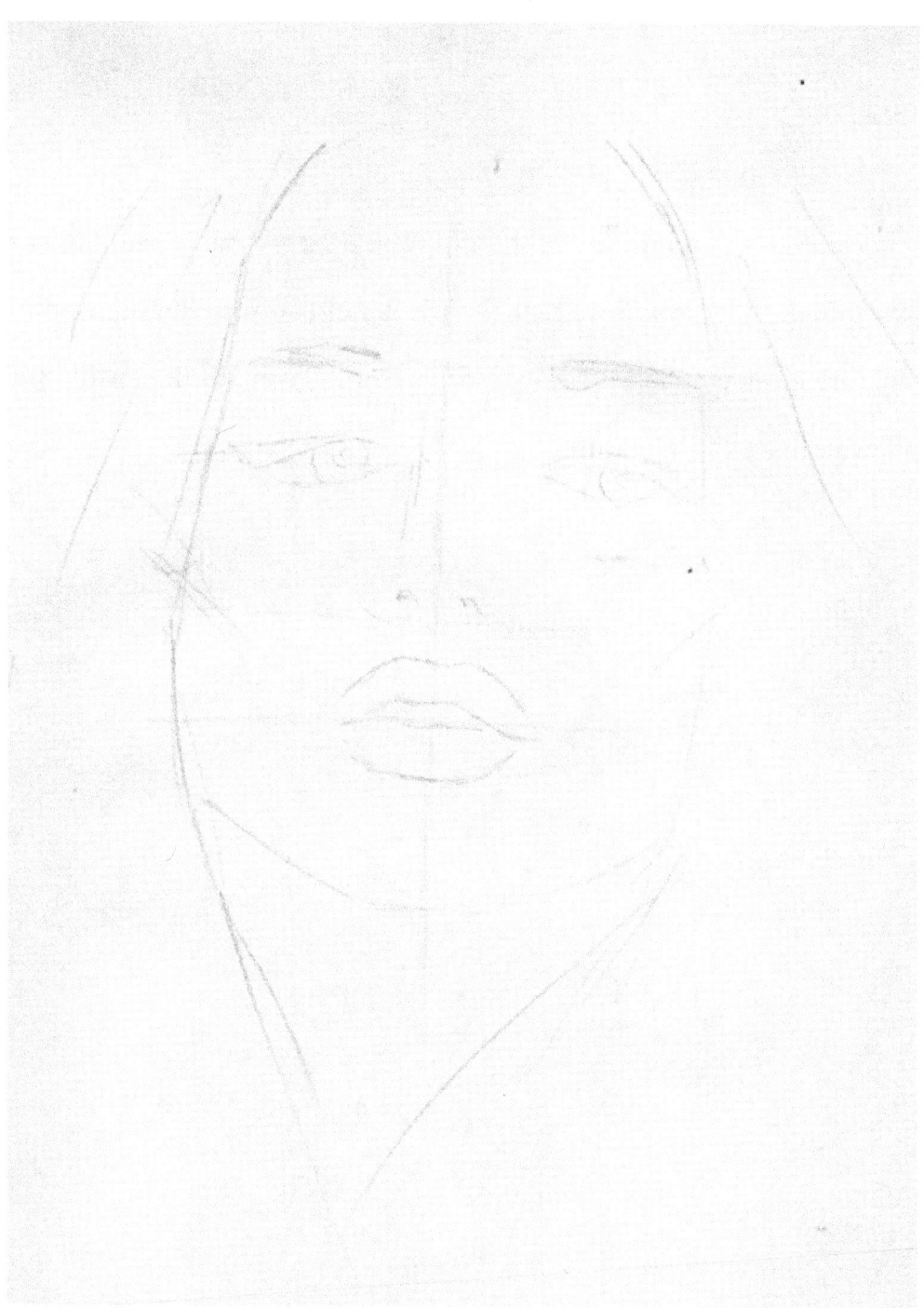

Step 2

Give details to the grim eyes of the girl. The eyes are half open and she is looking down sideways. Note that the iris is not completely visible and the eyelids are given emphasis. The eye socket is also given careful shading. The shading is given a light texture.

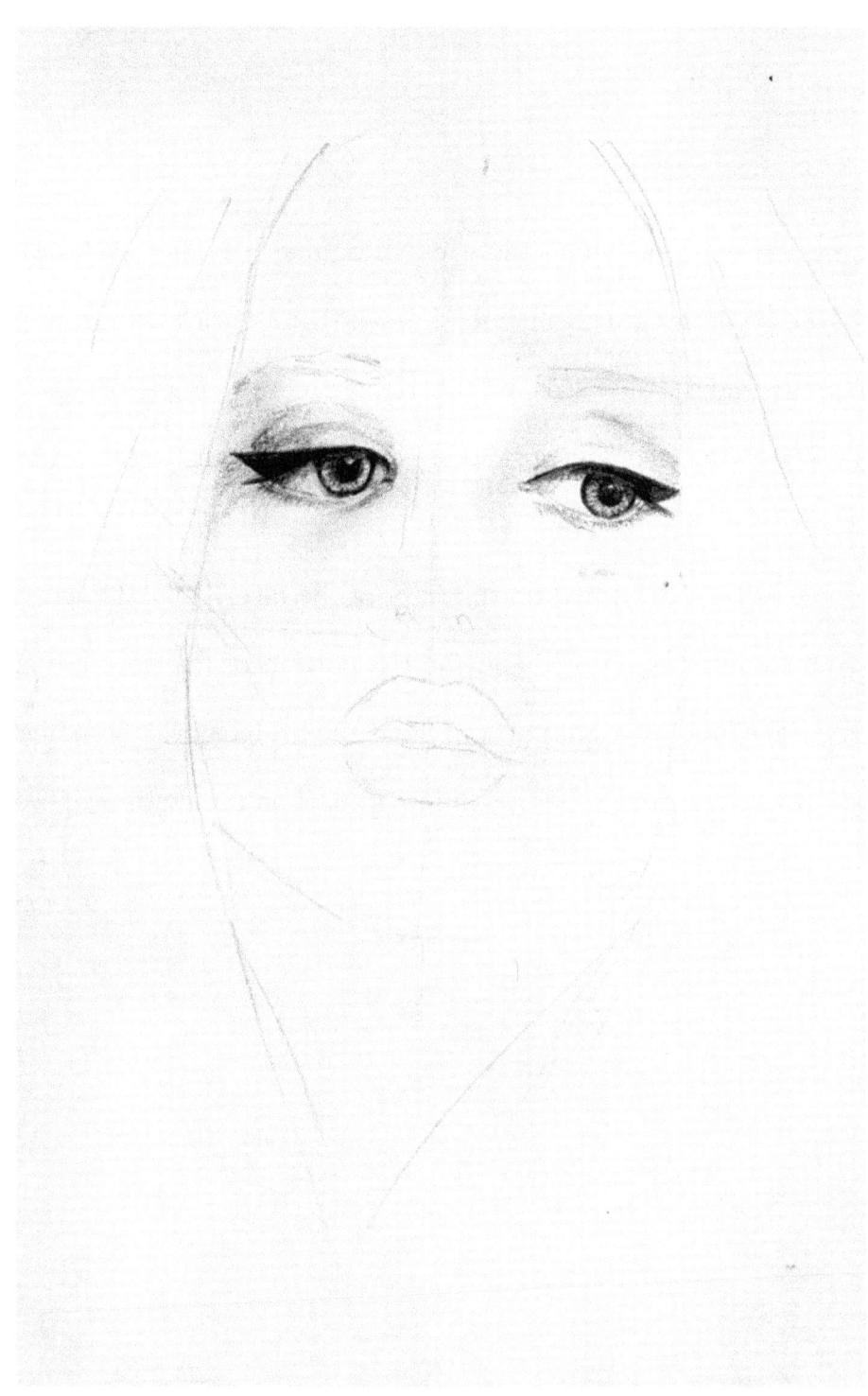

Step 3

After you are done sketching the eyes, draw the nose and eyebrows. The hairs of the eyebrows are given careful drawing in the right eyebrow. Notice the hair protruding outwards in the right eyebrow. Such details give a realistic look to the face. The nostrils are also drawn realistically, not ideally.

The source of light is located on the right of the face. Thus, the left side of the face including the left eye and the left portion of the nose are shaded slightly darker than the right portion. Since the bridge of the nose obstructs the eyes, the source of light has maximum impact on the shading of eyes and nose.

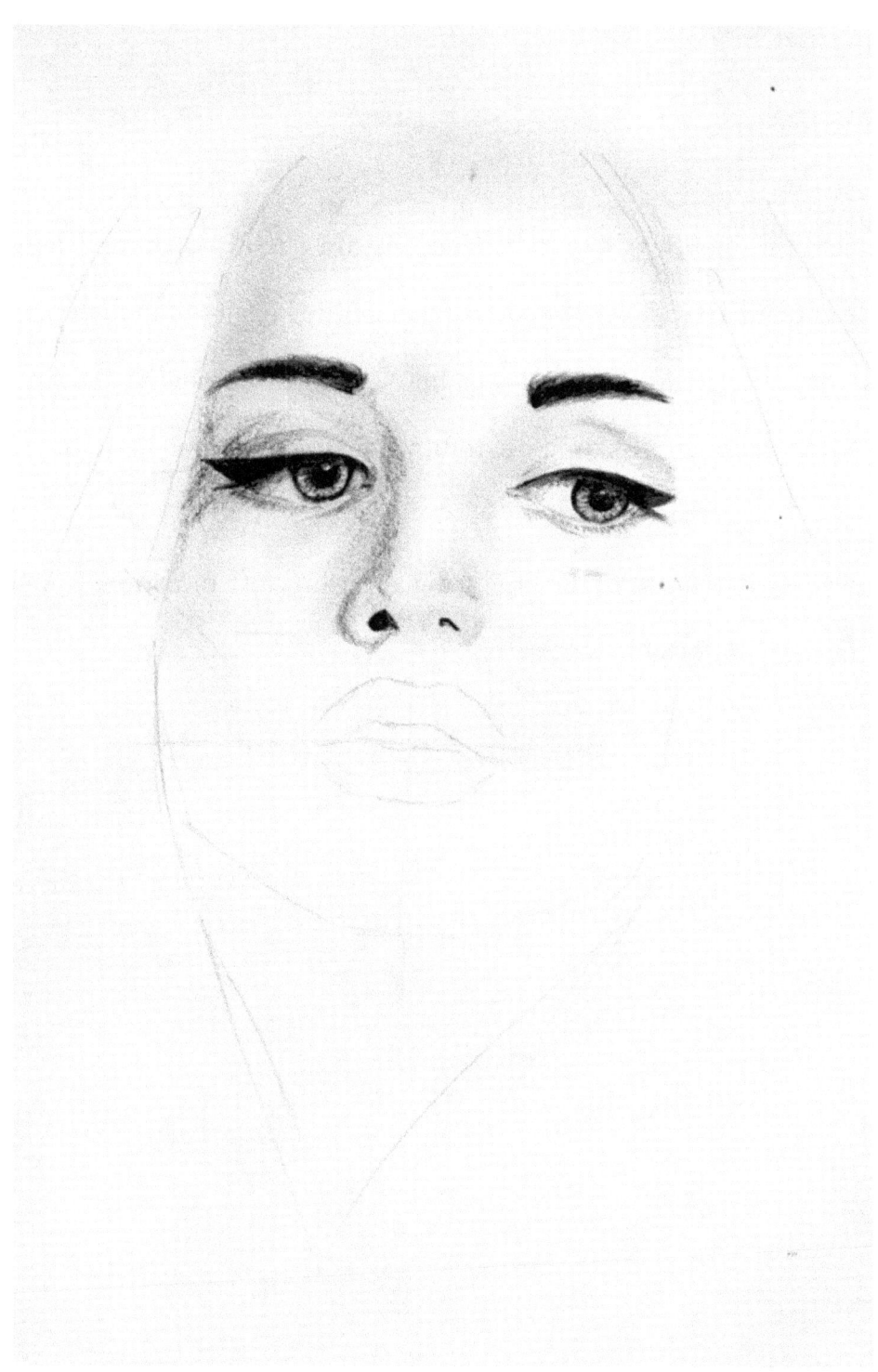

Step 4

Complete the mouth of the lady. The lips are slightly open and hence, a couple of teeth are visible. The lower lip is a little heavier than the upper lip. Thus, the inward curve of the lower lip is given prominence. The lips also have some cracks in the skin. Be careful while drawing these lines for cracks.

Give shading in the rest of the face using a muslin cloth or cotton, whichever tool you feel comfortable with.

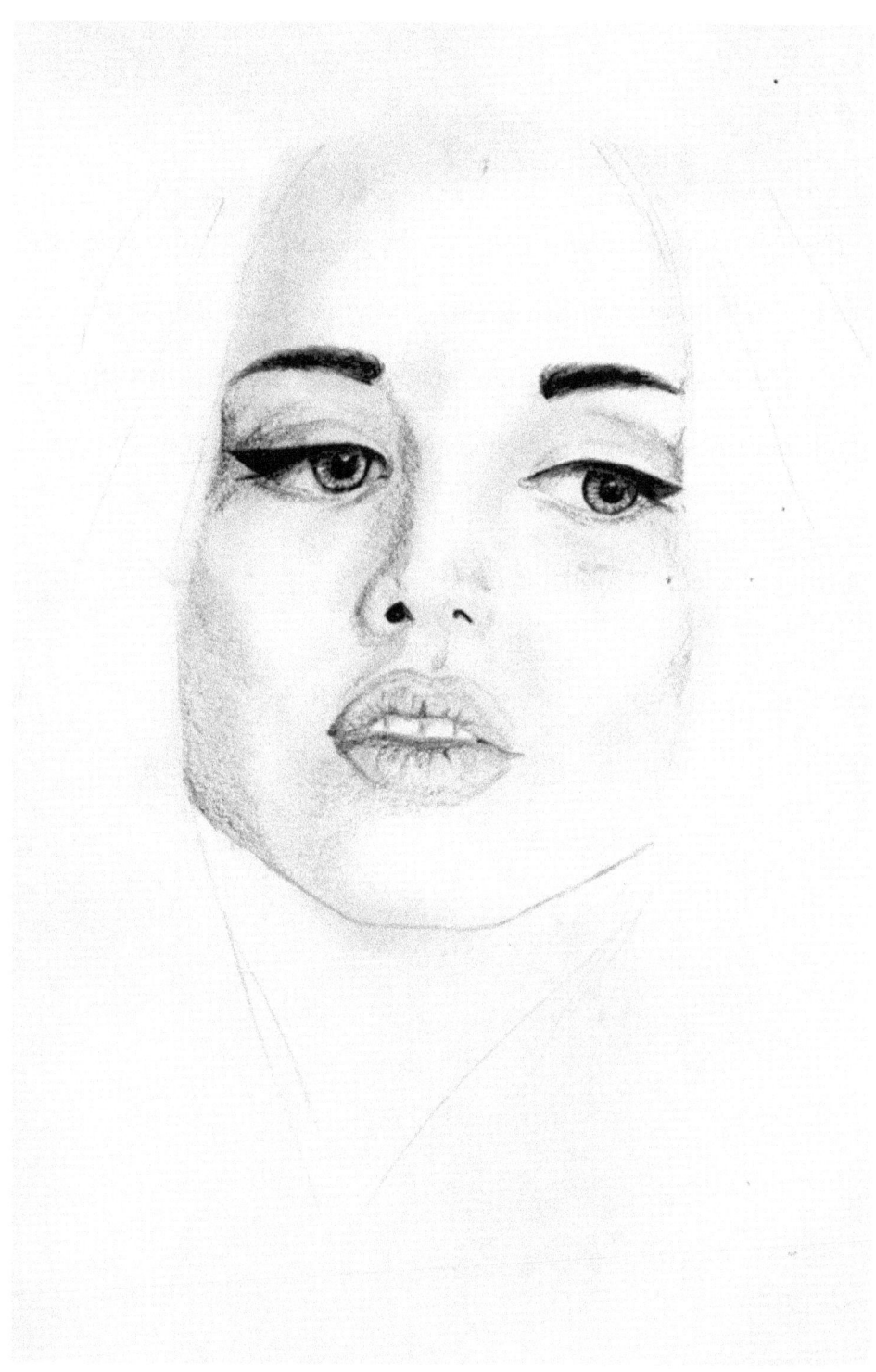

Step 5

Draw the hair falling on both sides of the face of this lady. Draw the hair strands in single undulating strokes only. Giving breaks in hairlines does not give a good look. When the hair fall on shoulders, the thickness and number of strands becomes lesser. The density of hair is maximum on the scalp.

The portrait of a female model is ready.

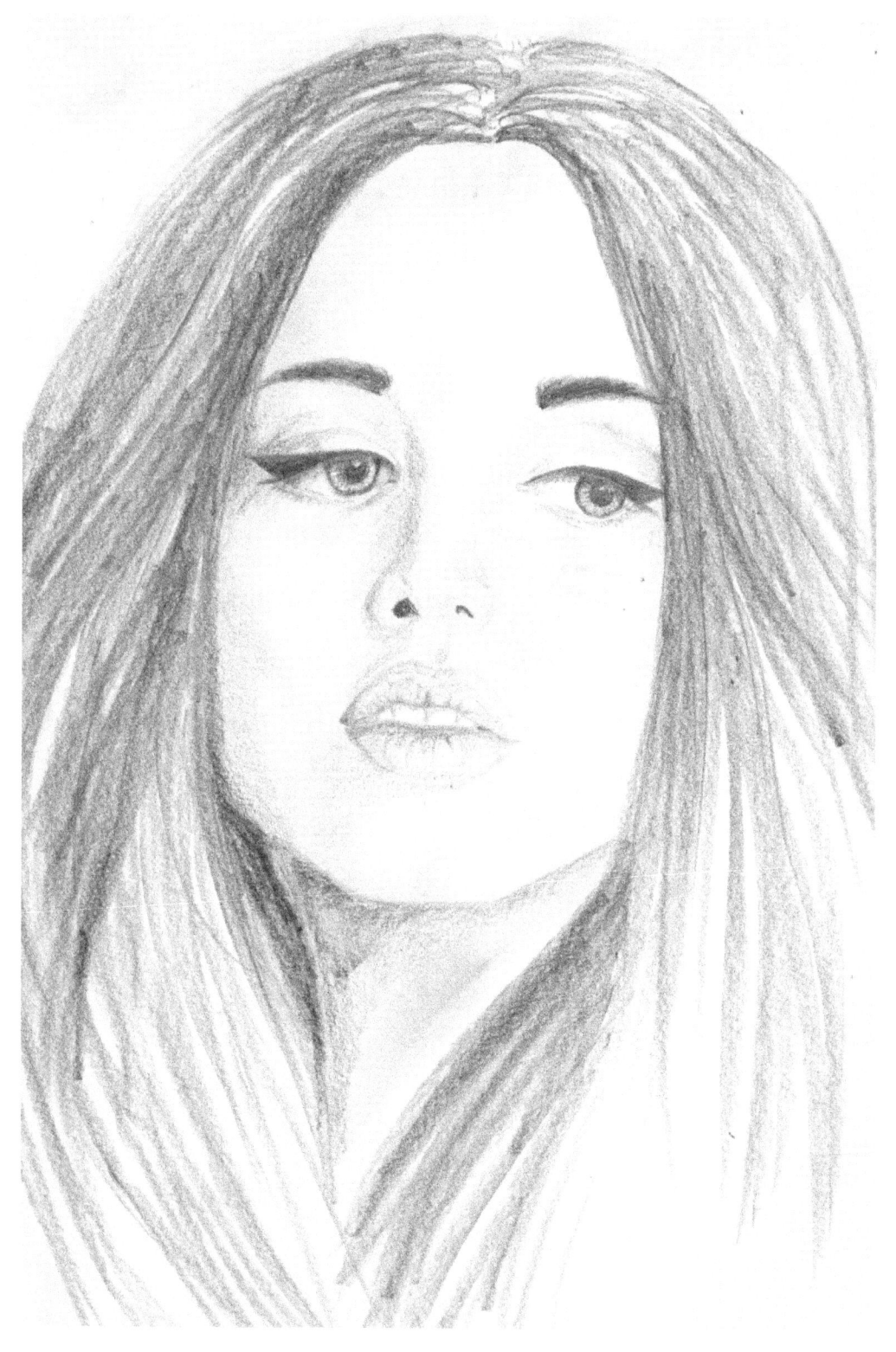

Chapter 2
How to Draw Portrait of a Bohemian Girl?

Step 1

In this chapter, we are going to draw the portrait of a bohemian girl. The face of this girl is tilted slightly sideways to the left. In the end, you will see that there is an intense, deep look in the eyes of this girl. While the face is tilted sideways, she is looking to the front. The girl is also wearing a headband, which can be drawn later. Her hairs are almost covering both the ears. Only the right earlobe is visible, with an earring hanging down.

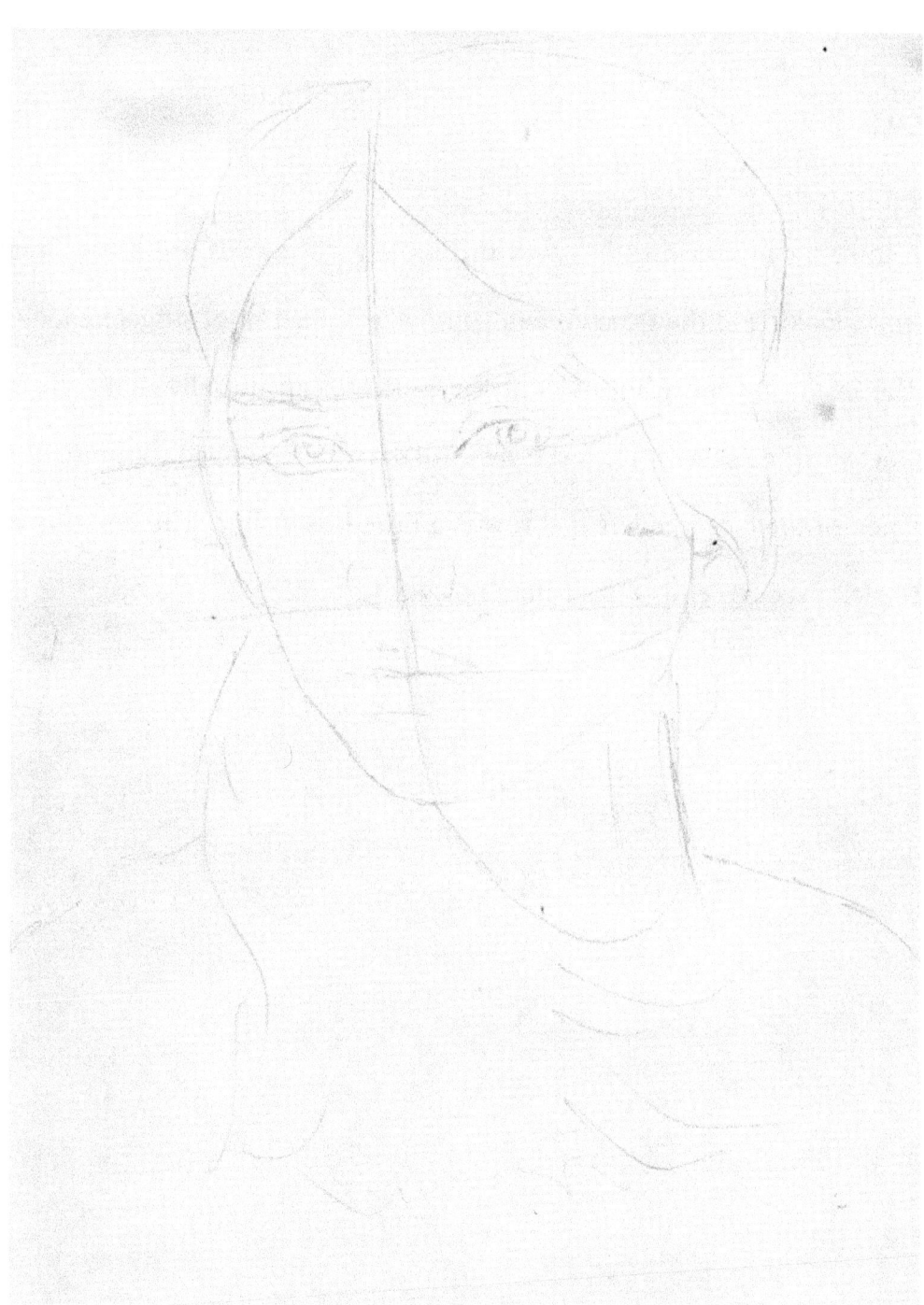

Step 2

Let us begin by drawing the eyes of this lady. The eyes are shown really intense, looking in the front. When you make a portrait of someone looking in the front, anyone who looks at the portrait can literally make an eye-contact with the sketch. The eyebrows are drawn arc-shaped. Because of the position of the face, the left eyebrow is a little less visible. The tapering end of the left eyebrow ends earlier than normal.

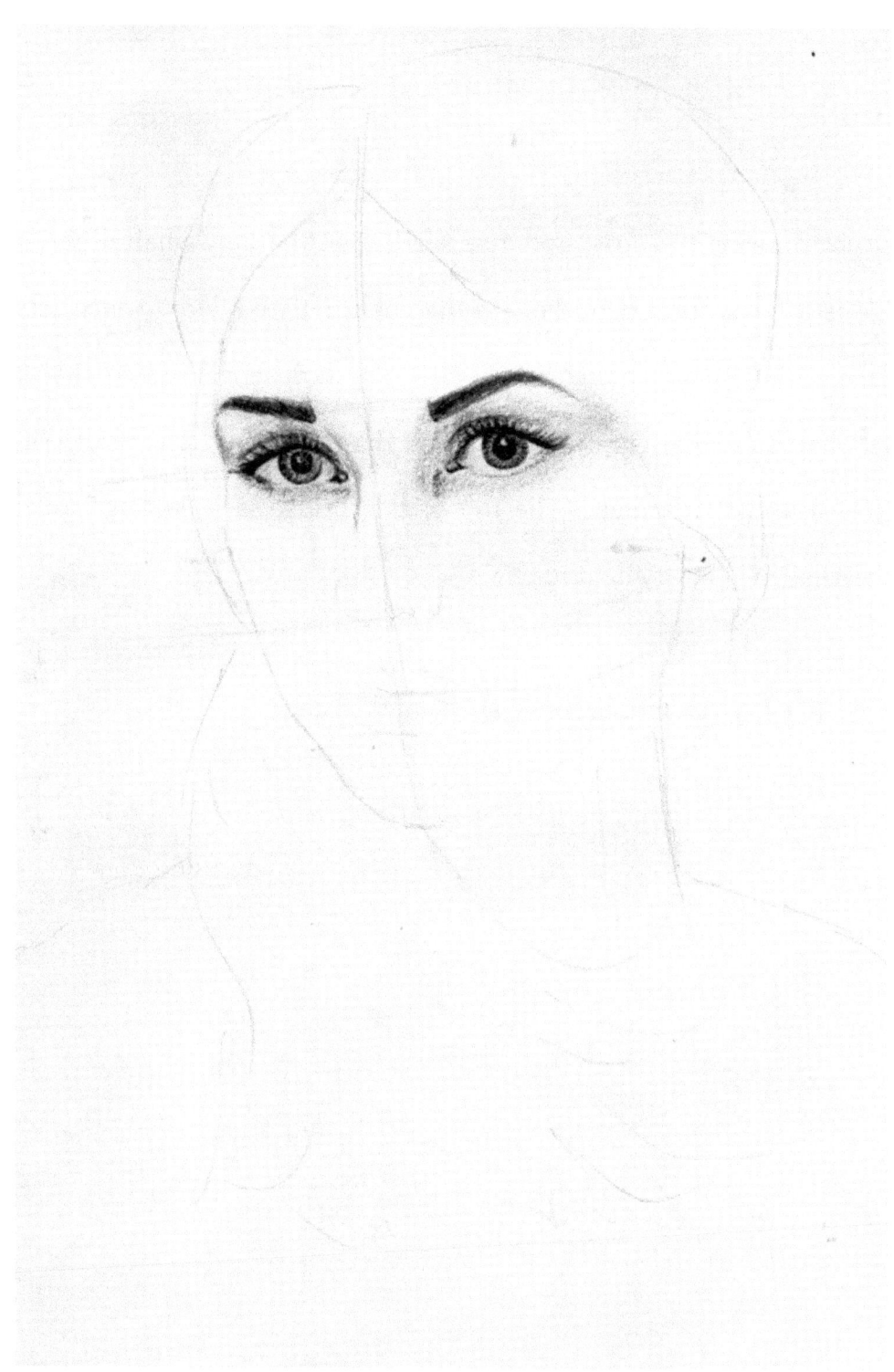

Step 3

Begin by drawing the nose, and give shading in the upper half of the face. There is a beautiful indentation in the cheeks of this lady, which lets us make a variation in shading in the face. The nose is also tilted sideways, which makes one nostril more prominent than the other. The bridge of the nose is beautifully straight. The top of this bridge is reflecting light and hence, shaded in a very light tone.

The jaw line is given more refined shape in this step.

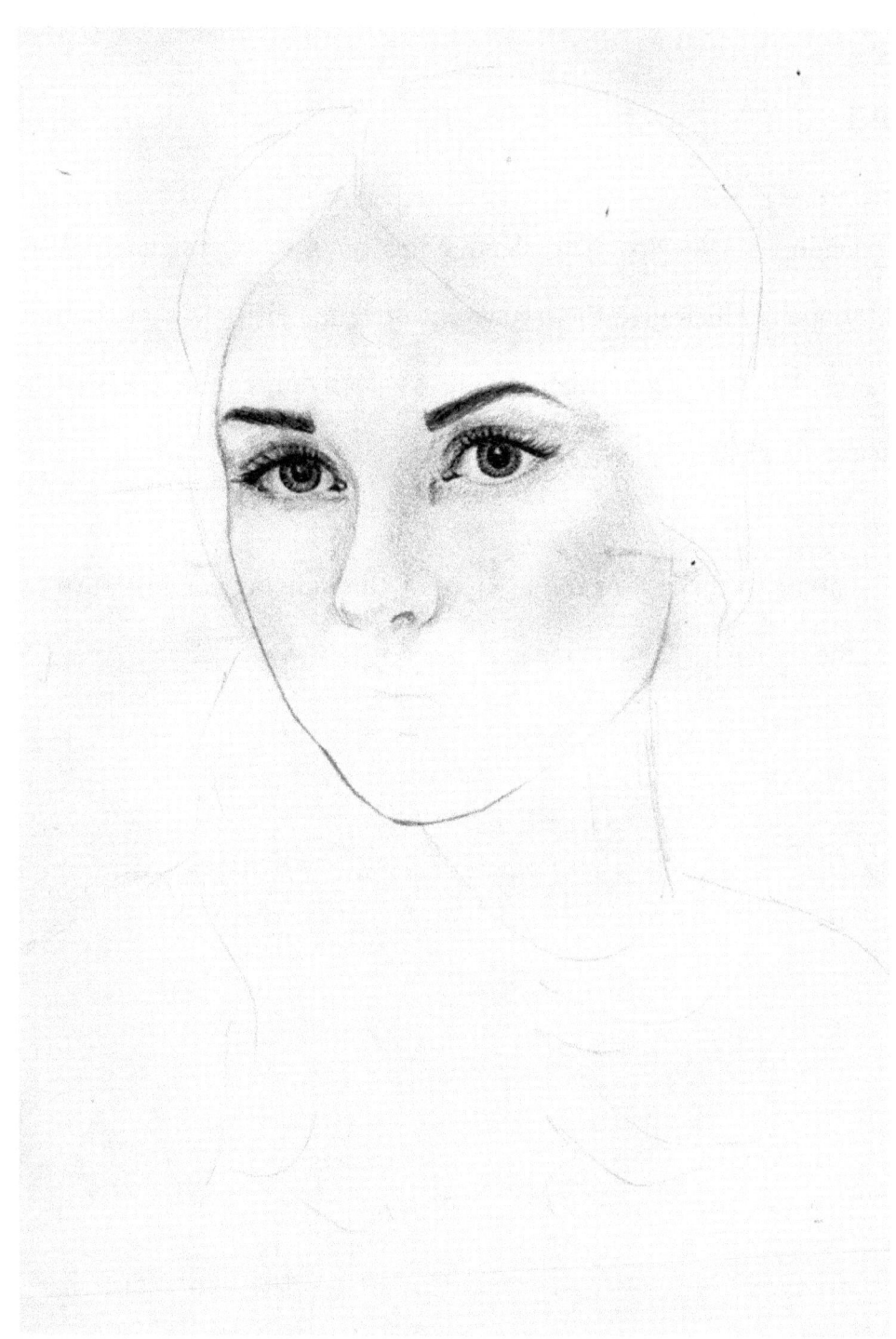

Step 4

Give shading in the lips. The slender lips of this bohemian girl are very slightly open, which give the appearance of thoughtfulness in conjunction with eyes. The opening between the lips is given darker shading because the teeth are not visible.

Give shading in the rest of the face. Draw the hanging earring worn by the girl in the right ear. The earlobe is also very slightly visible.

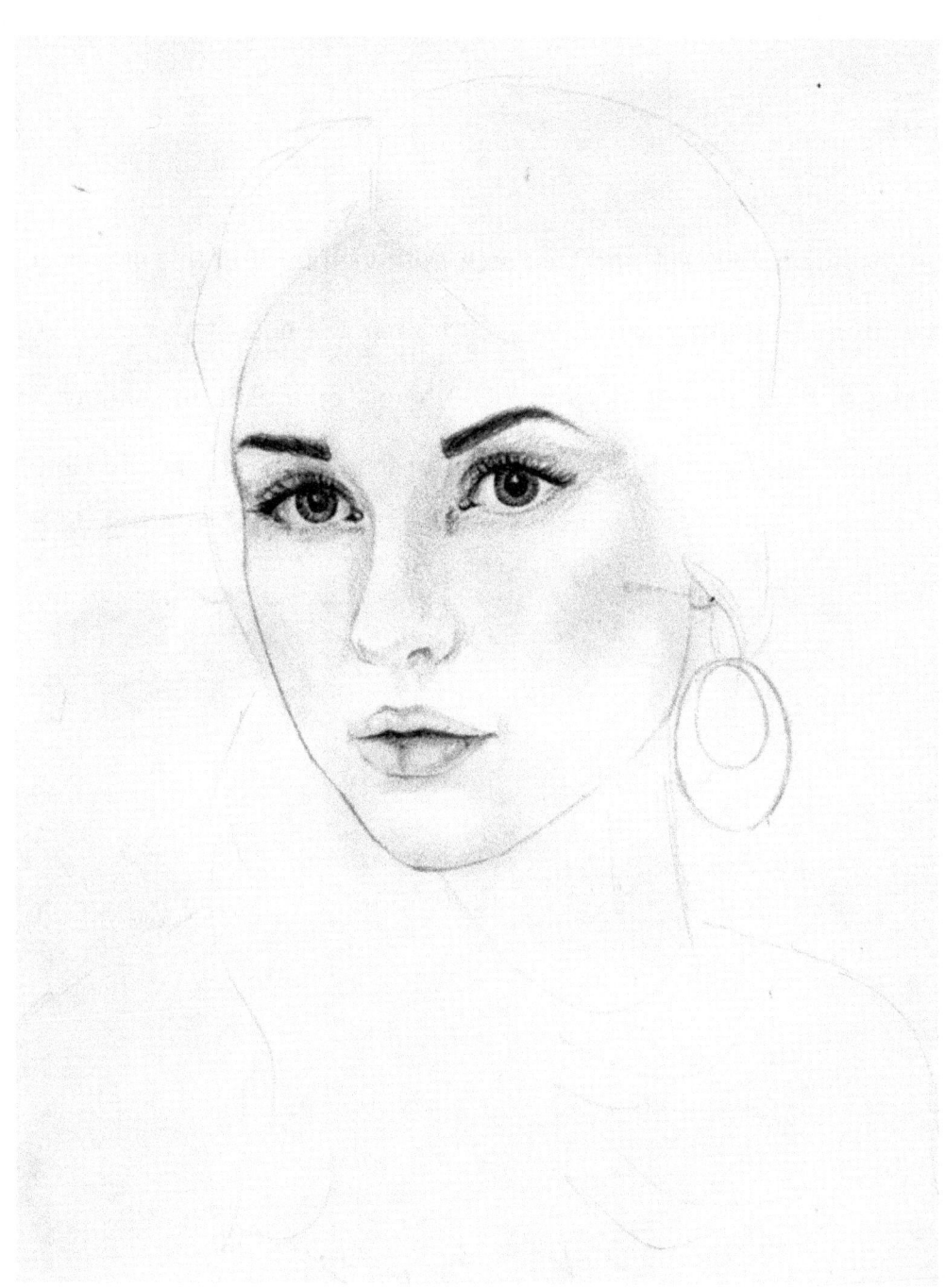

Step 5

Give shading in the neck and bust area. Although most of this area is going to be covered with hair, which we will draw in the next step; we are giving shading so that this area does not look empty or broken in shading later. The willowy neck of this girl is given careful shading in vertical direction.

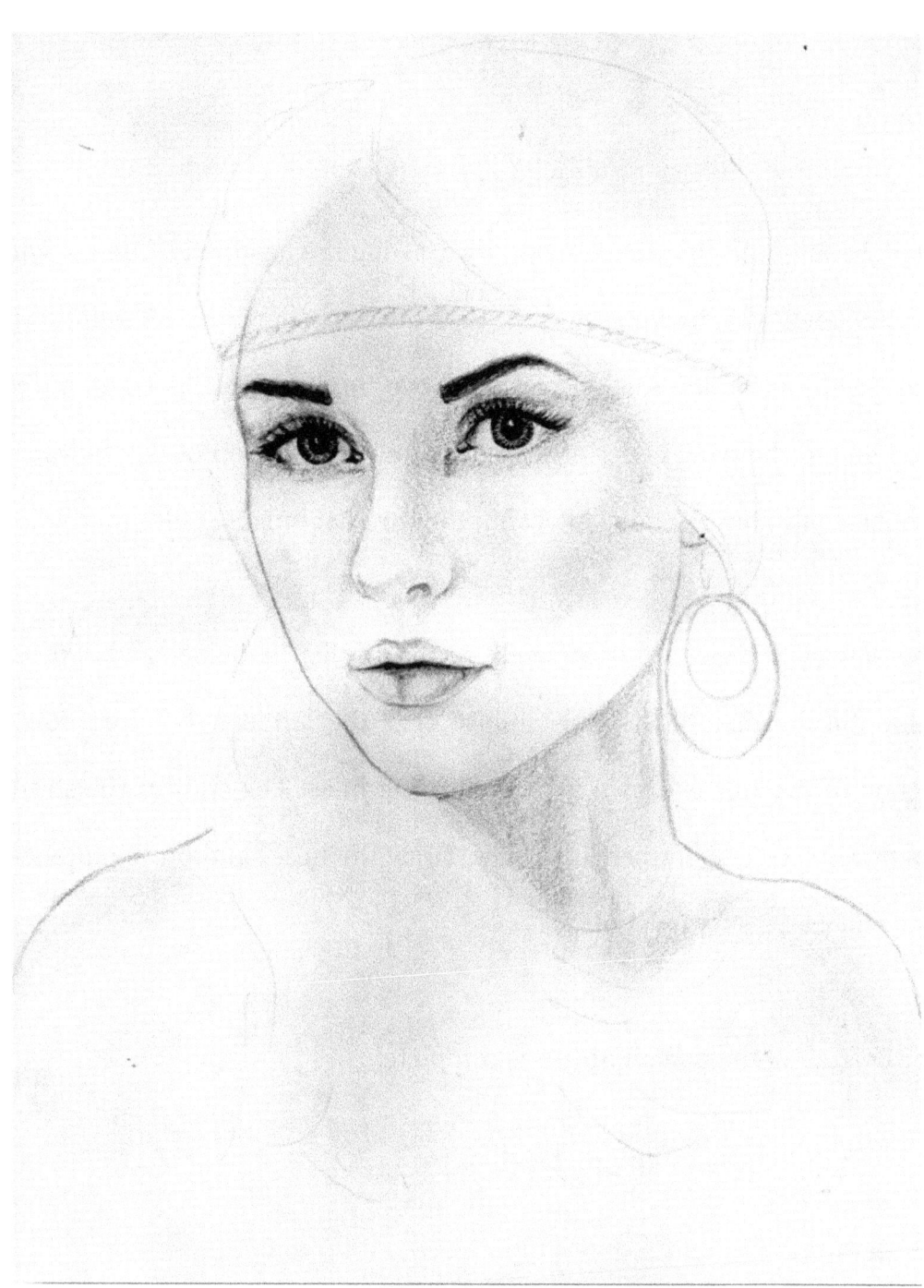

Step 6

Draw hairs of the girl. Leave space for drawing the headband. Draw it when you are done with drawing the hair. Give heavy shading and smooth flowing lines in the hair. The section of hair above the headband is bulging out a little due to the tying effect of the headband. The section of hair below the headband also has the tying effect but they are not bulging out.

The hair of this girl are completely set on the left shoulder and set loose below the headband. Starting almost near the left ear, the free flowing section of the hair is drawn with undulating lines. The ends of the strands are drawn free ends of pencil strokes. Draw the headband on the forehead. Draw the earring with details.

The portrait of the bohemian girl is complete.

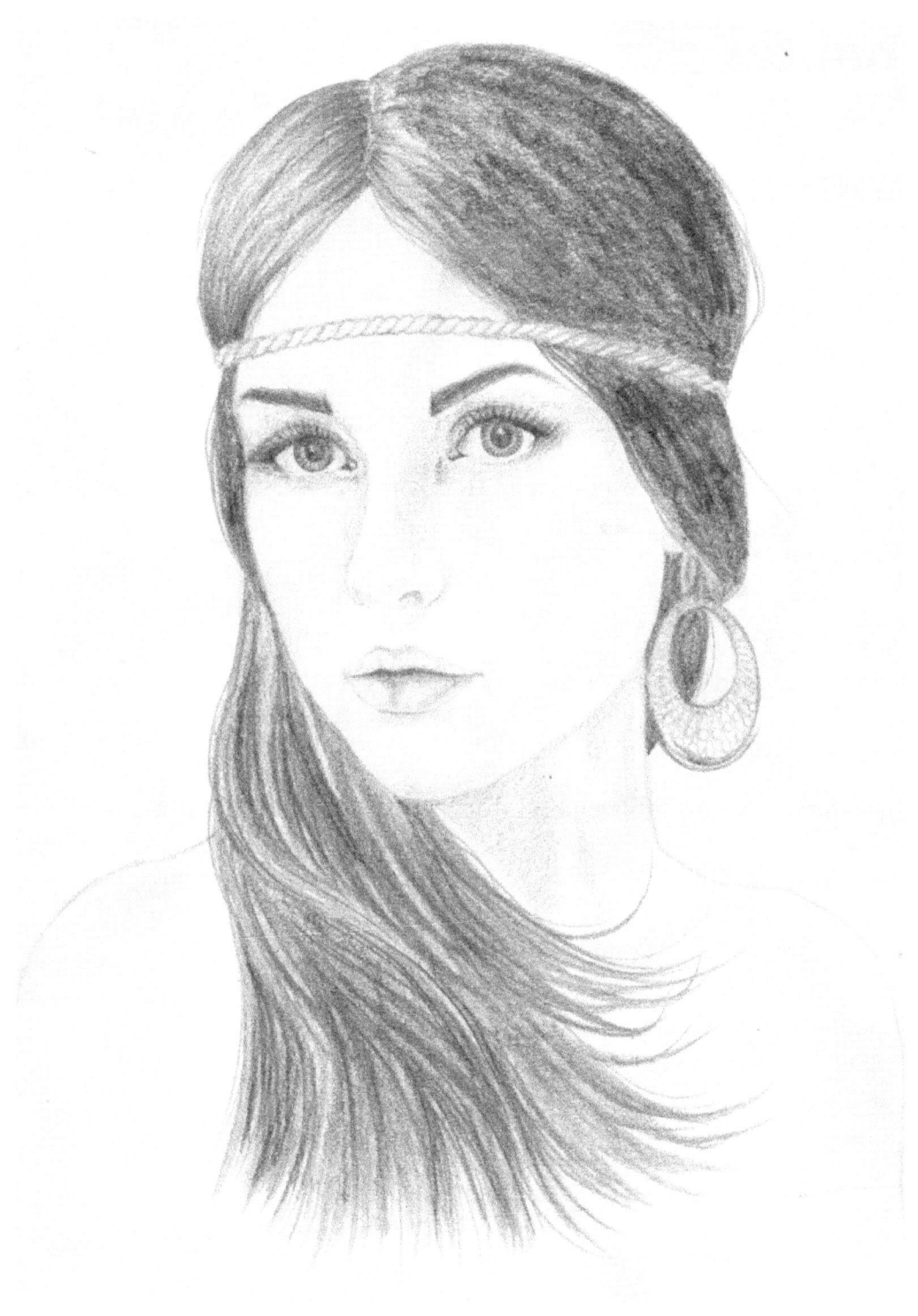

Chapter 3
How to Draw Portrait of a Male Model?

Step 1

In this chapter, we are going to draw the portrait of a male model, whose face has been given more emphasis than the hairs. This is the portrait in profile of this boy.

Draw the basic outline of the boy's face. He is looking sideways and slightly upwards. The jaw line is very sharp and the hairs are fuller in density. Some of the hairs are also falling on the forehead. Draw the outlines of these features accordingly.

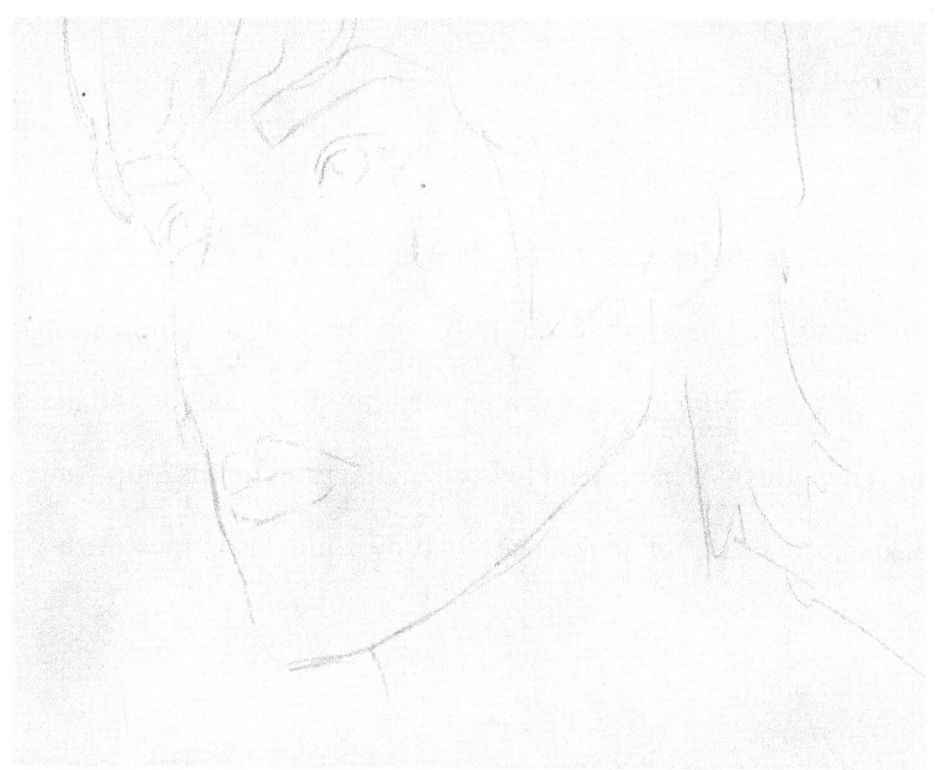

Step 2

Draw and shade the eyes of the boy looking sideways. The left eye is much less visible to the viewer than the right eye because of the position of the face. The details of the eyes are drawn very carefully. Look at the upper and lower eyelids, the hair have been twisted vigilantly. The iris, pupil and sclera are also given beautiful look. The eyebrows are also thick with a good density of hairs.

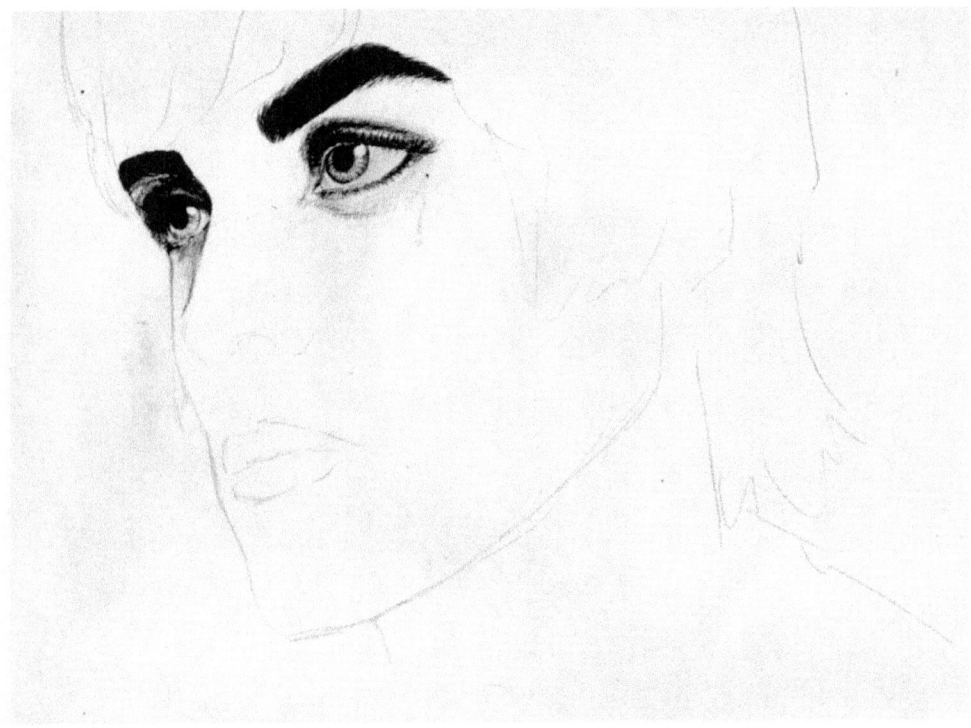

Step 3

Give shading in the area around the eyes and nose. Draw the nose with its bridge tapering straight downwards. Only one nostril is visible because of the position of the face. The nostril in the profile is shown arc-shaped.

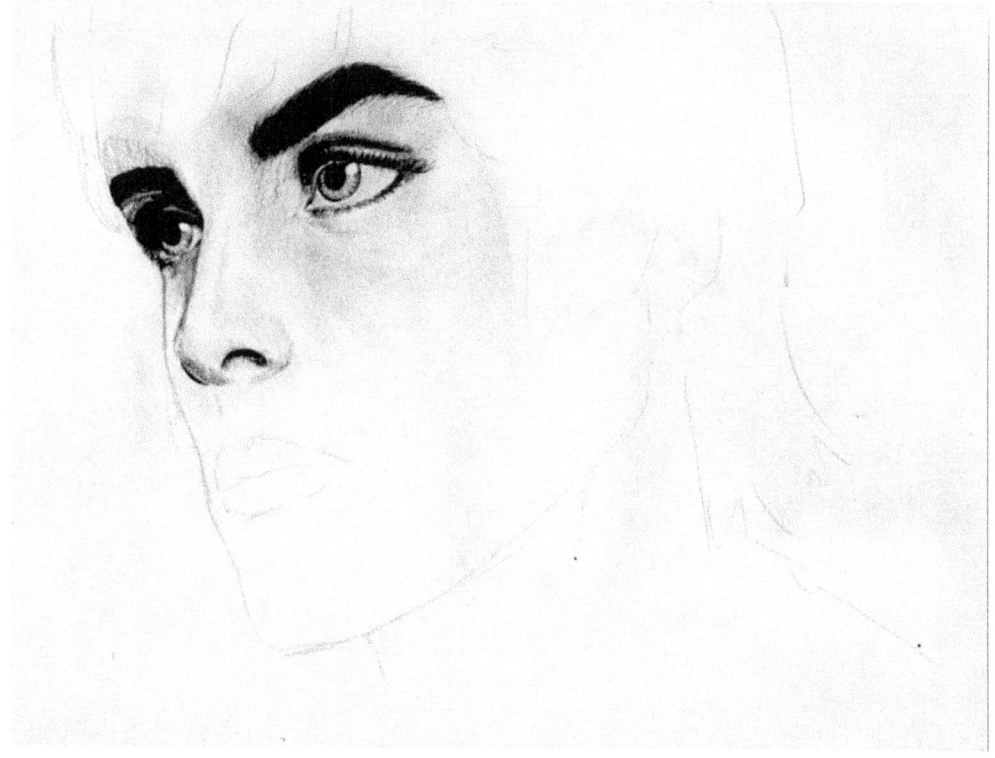

Step 4

Draw the lips of the boy. Since he is not shown smiling, the lips are enclosed. The lines of the lips are prominently visible. The joining line of the lips is darkened. This joining line is never straight, as the common perception of the most artists is. There is a fine indentation below the center of the nose.

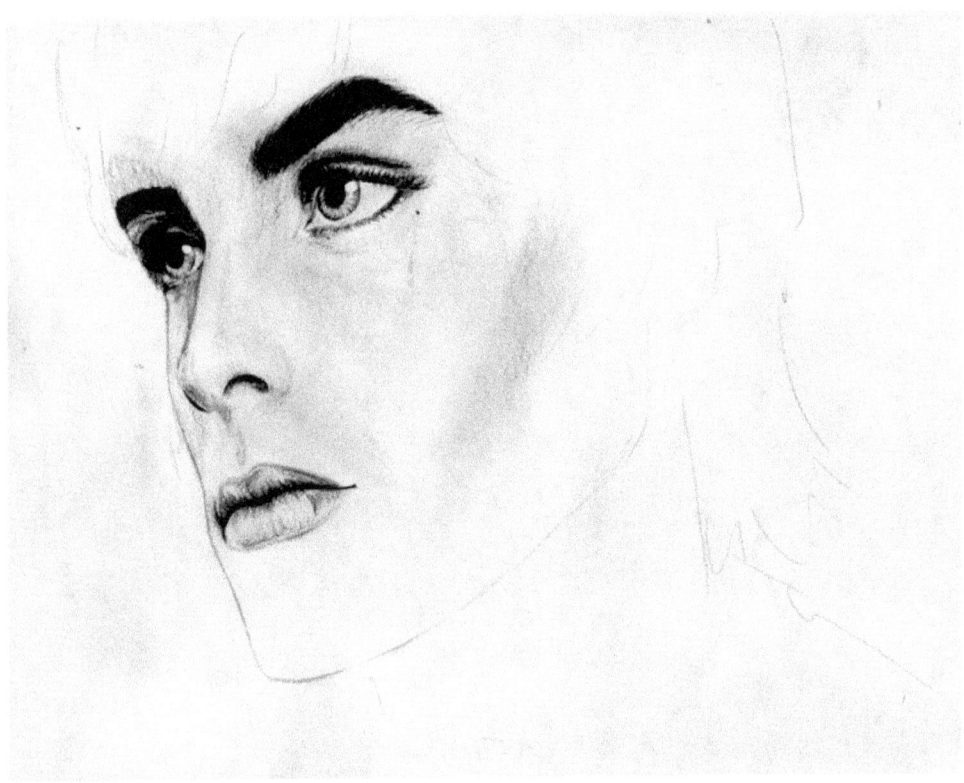

Step 5

After giving shading in the face, draw the hair for stubble. The hairs form a very important feature on a man's face. Thus, you must draw these hairs very watchfully. Give shading in the neck and just below the chin. A very few hairs are shown below the chin as well. Give a suggestion of the collar of the shirt.

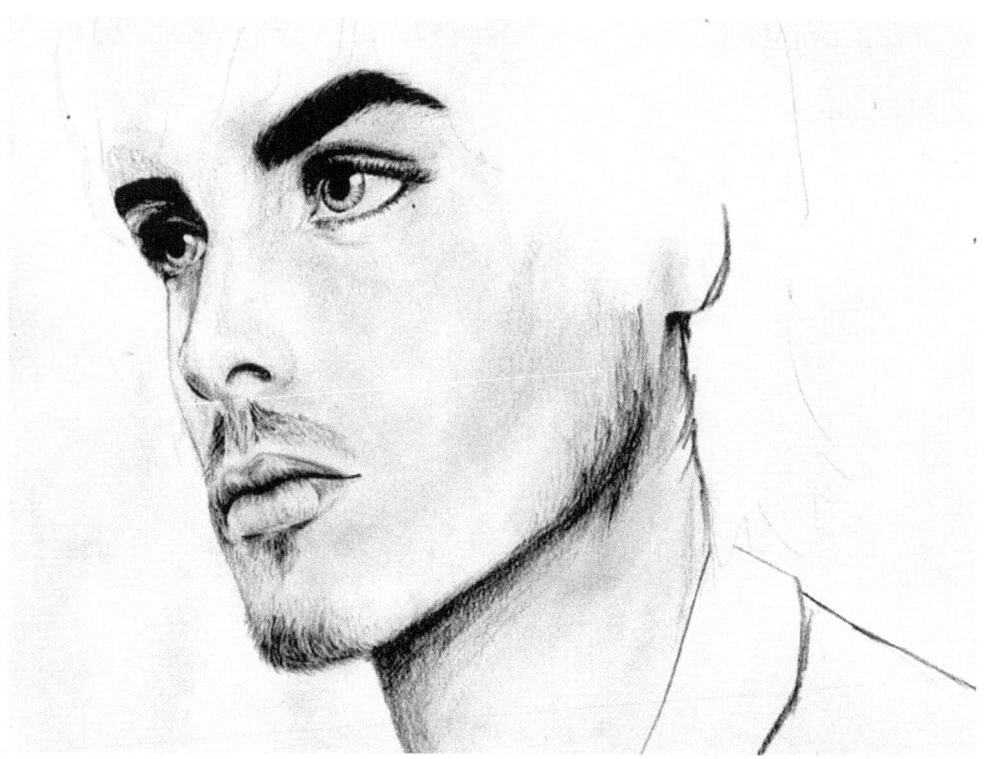

Step 6

Draw and shade the hair of the boy. Like the hair of the stubble, the hair on the head also form an equally important part of a man's portrait. Give these hairs a fuller density and a fall on the face. The hairs also falling on the side of the face near the ear. The earlobe is visible out of the hairs. The hairs are also falling on the neck.

Give shading in the garment of the boy. The portrait in profile of the male model is ready.

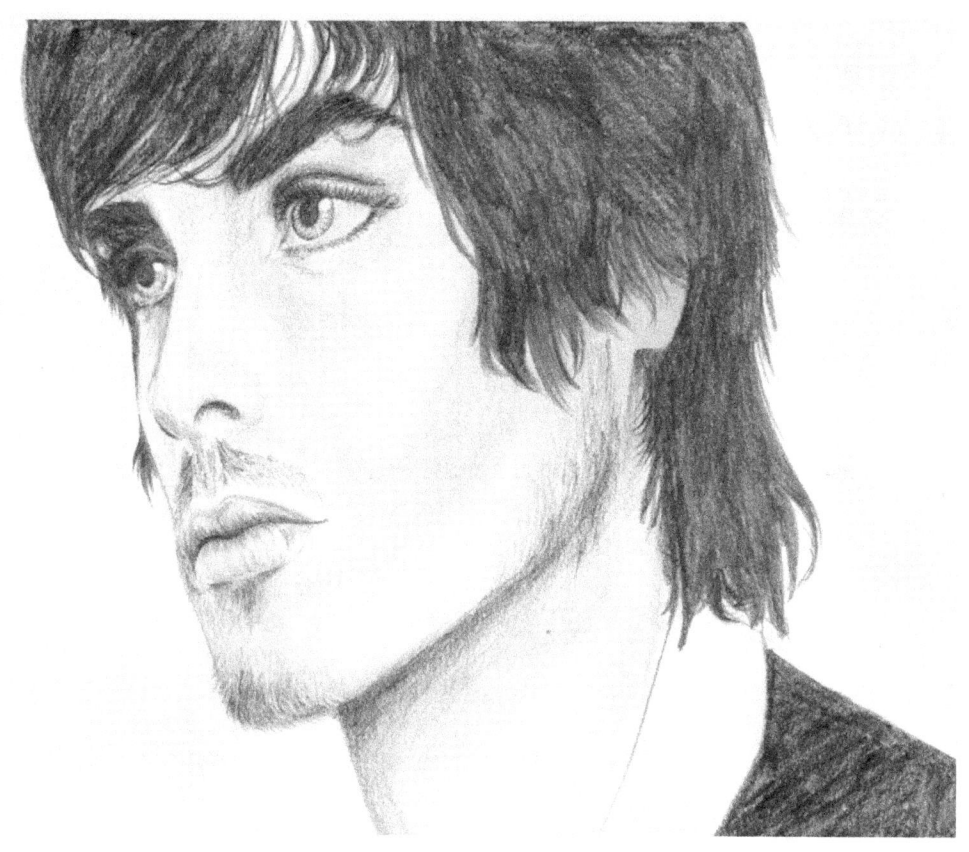

Chapter 4
How to Draw a Girl with a Spear?

Step 1

Here, we will draw a girl carrying a spear. Since the girl is a fighter, her body has a significant presence of muscles. Draw the outline of the body. One hand is resting on the waist and the other is hanging down carrying the spear. The spear will be drawn later. Notice a few lines drawn on the limbs of the girl. They are drawn as guides for drawing muscles later.

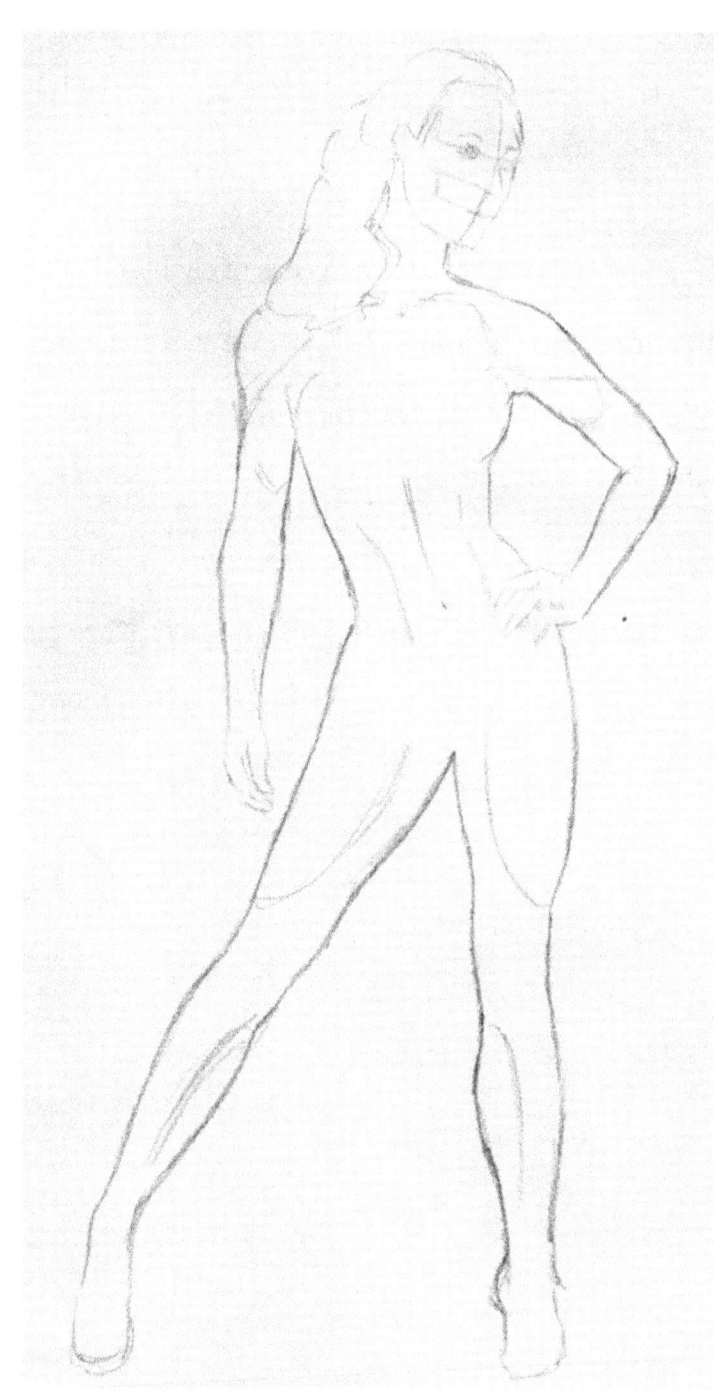

Step 2

When we draw a portrait, we have to take care of each and every detail of the face. But, while drawing full human figures, we can focus less on face and give our attention to the whole body of the human.

Draw the features of the face including eyes, nose, mouth, ear (since the profile of the face is visible). The expressions on the face are gloomy.

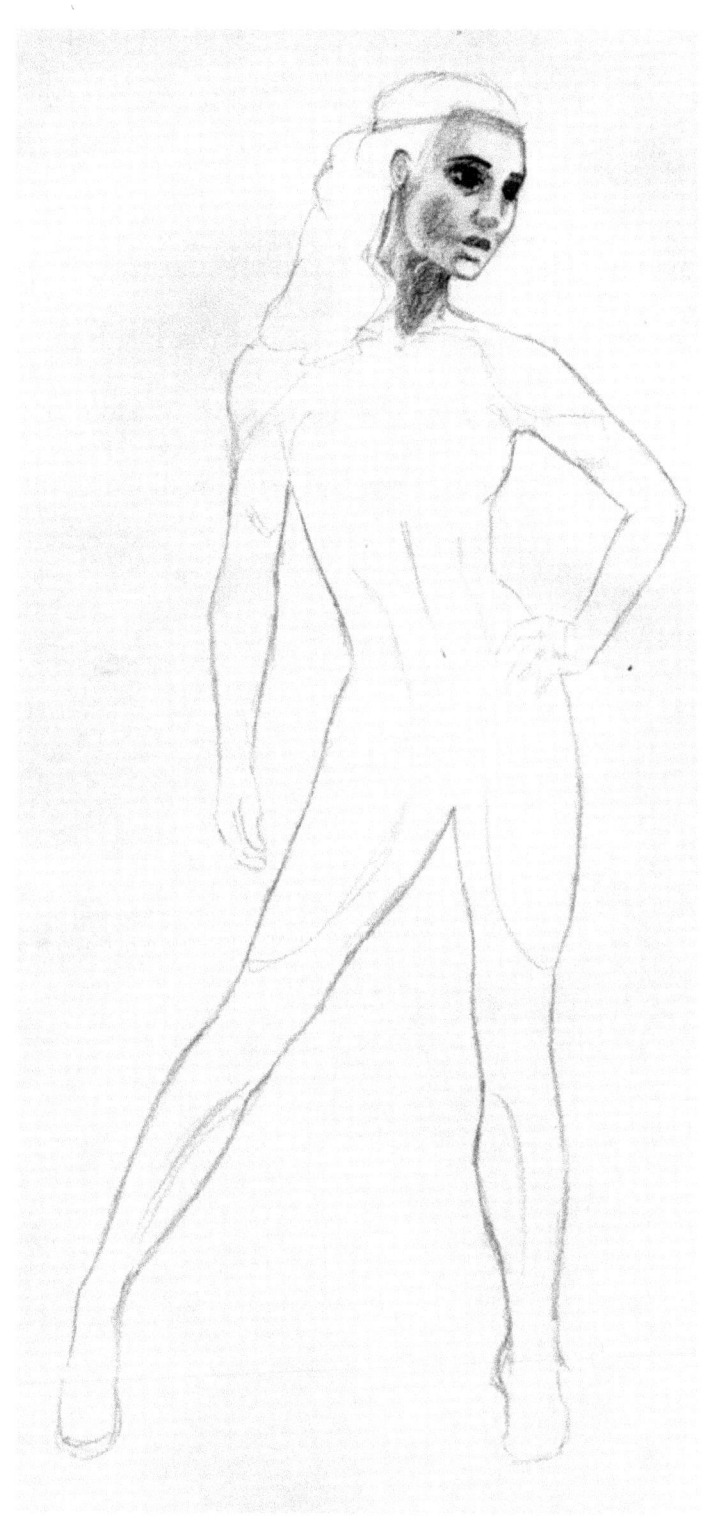

Step 3

The girl is shown in briefs. Draw the garments and leave them for shading later. Draw the hairs tied nicely at the back of the head and some of them are falling on the left shoulder. The hairs have a wavy quality in them. Complete the shading in the bust area and arms, which are muscular.

Draw the spear in the left arm.

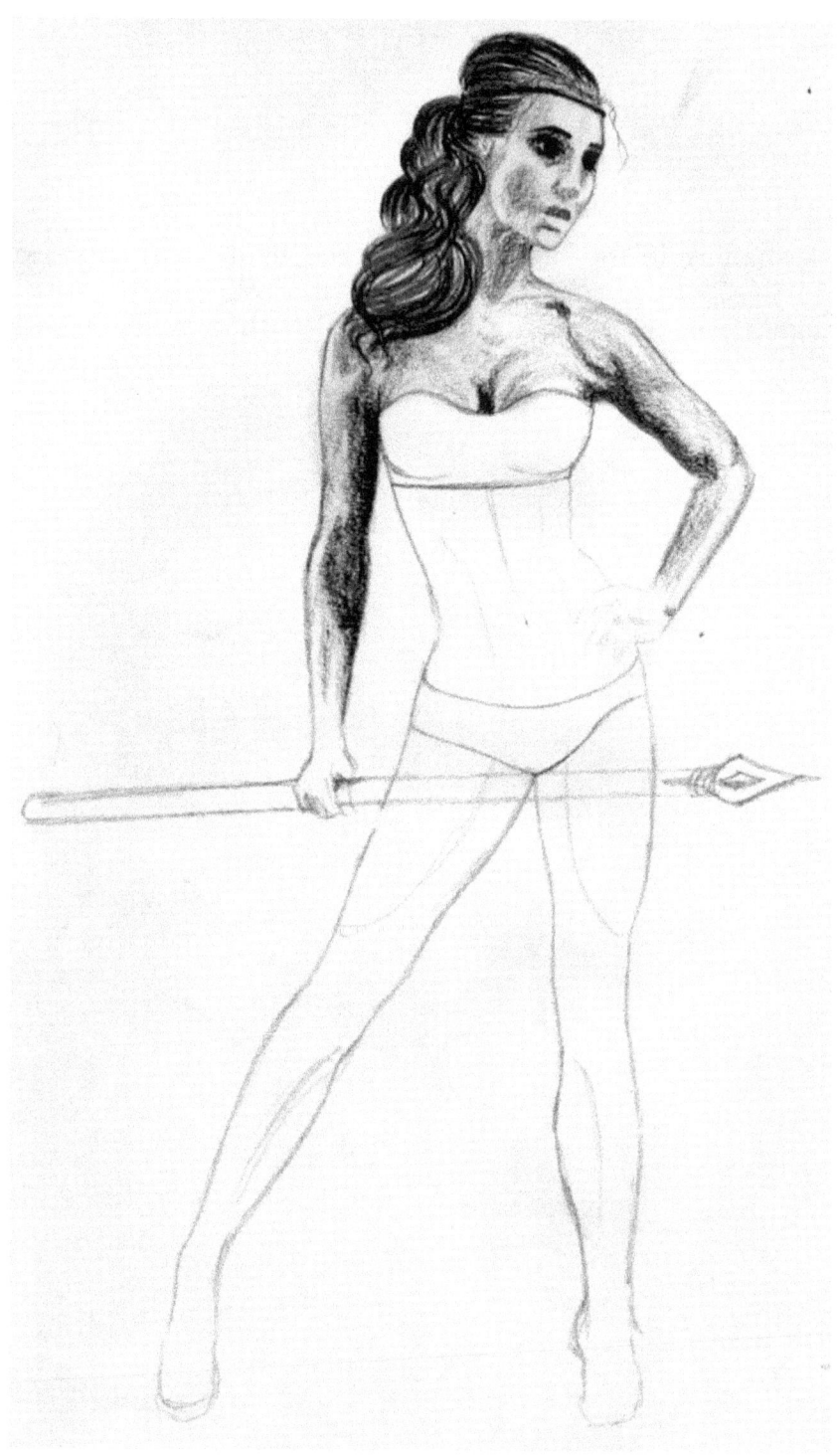

Step 4

Give dark shading in the briefs worn by the fighter girl. Also, shade the abdomen giving details of the muscles. Complete the shading in both hands.

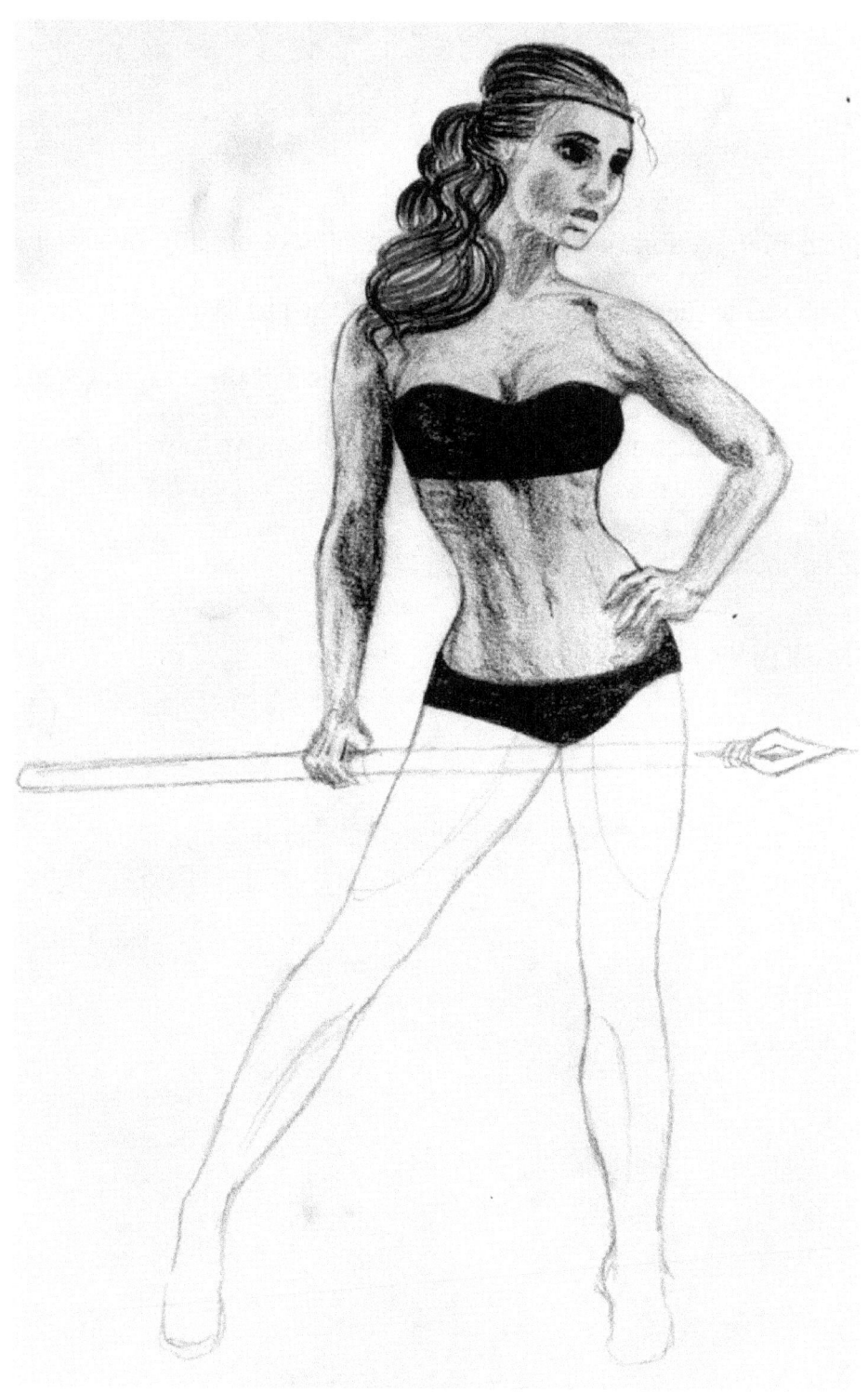

Step 5

Complete the shading in the legs giving details of slightly heavy muscles. Draw and shade the spear in the left hand of the girl. Also, draw the strings barefoot sandals of the girl. Since it is a front view of the body of the girl, the heels or soles of the sandals are hardly visible. Just give a suggestion of soles below the feet.

The sketch of the girl with a spear is complete.

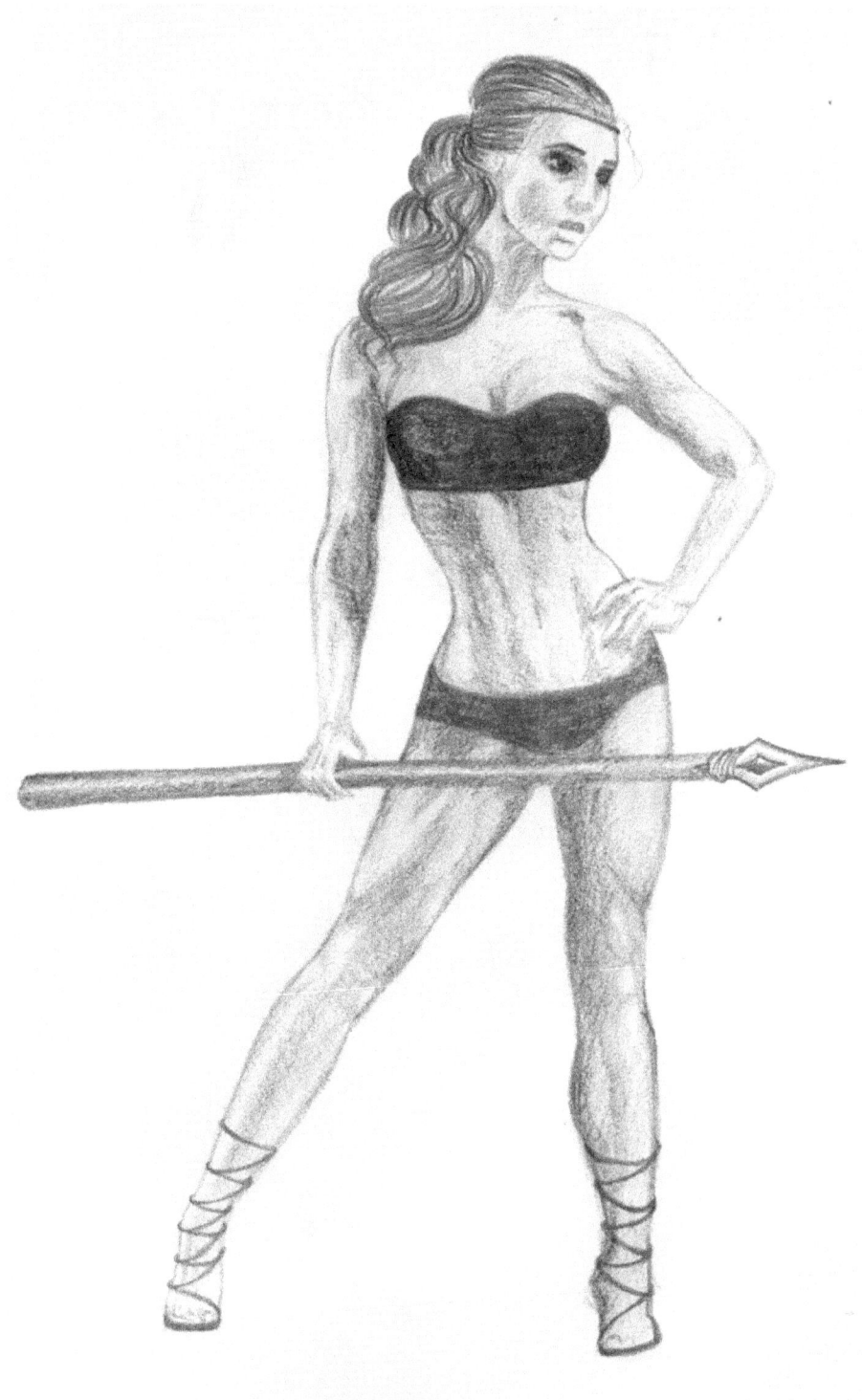

Chapter 5
How to Draw a Lady in Formals?

Step 1

We are going to draw a girl wearing formal clothes and having swirling loose hair. One hand of hers is resting on her waist and the other hand is hanging loose. Notice the circles drawn at various points in her body. They have been drawn to show some joints and bones.

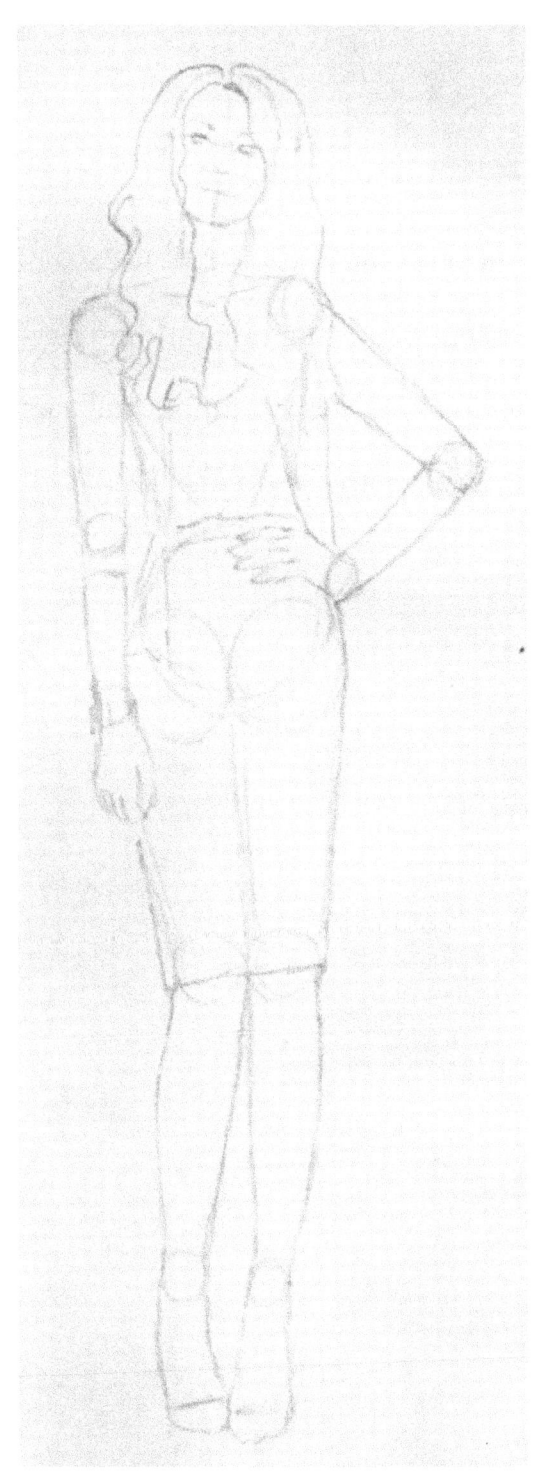

Step 2

Like we did in the previous sketch, we will focus lesser on the details of the face and instead distribute our attention on drawing the complete figure. Draw the suggestions for eyes, nose and lips. The ears are covered by the curly hairs hanging loose on both sides of the face.

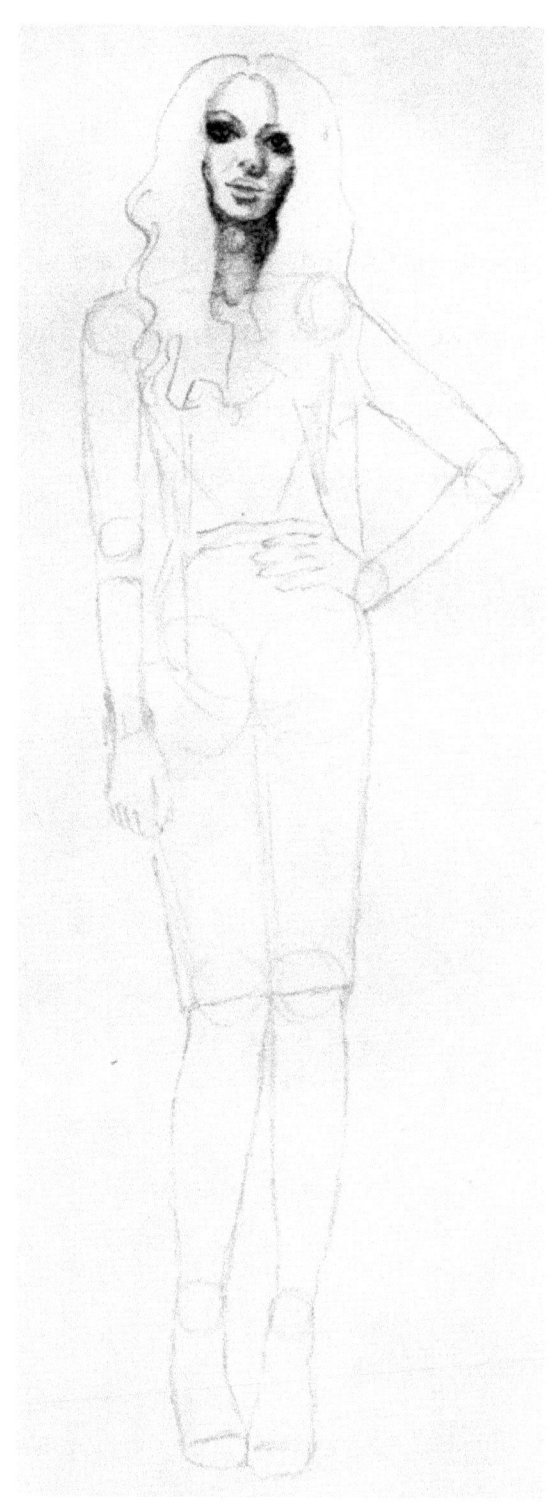

Step 3

Draw the upper garments of the lady consisting of a top and a coat, whose sleeves are gathered upwards. Notice the emphasis given on the crumpled sleeves of the coat and the beautiful effect emerging out of it. Also, draw a chain with a pendant hanging along the neck of the lady.

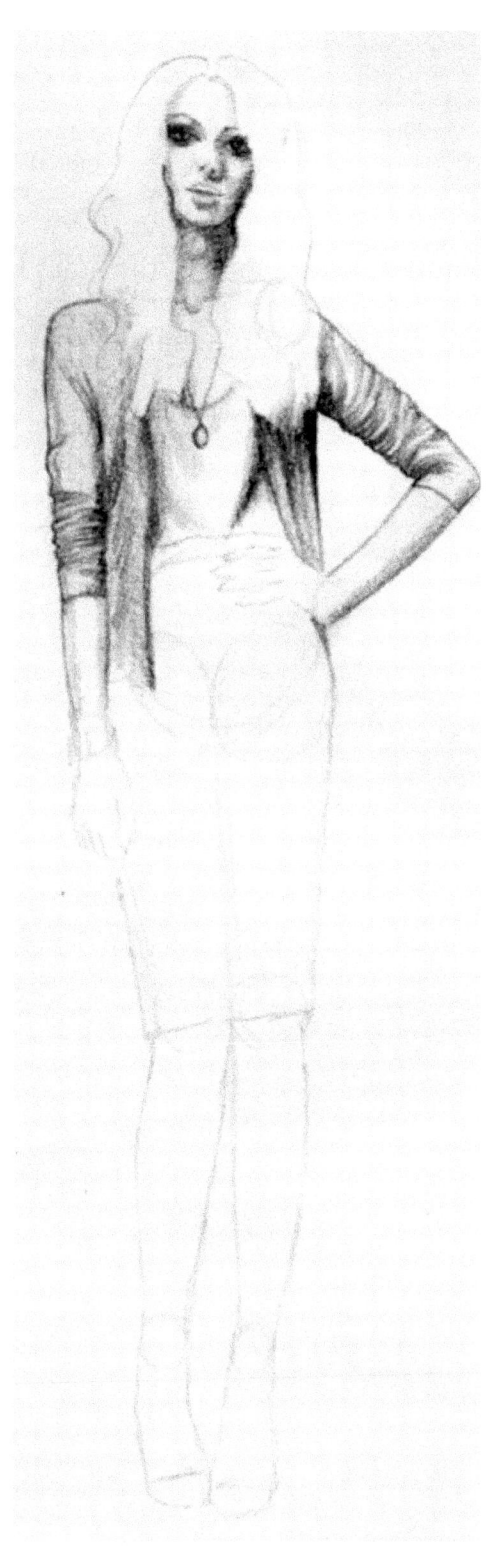

Step 4

Give shading in the beautiful beach curls of the hairs hanging loose on both shoulders. The hairs are drawn in such a manner that they give depth to the face as well.

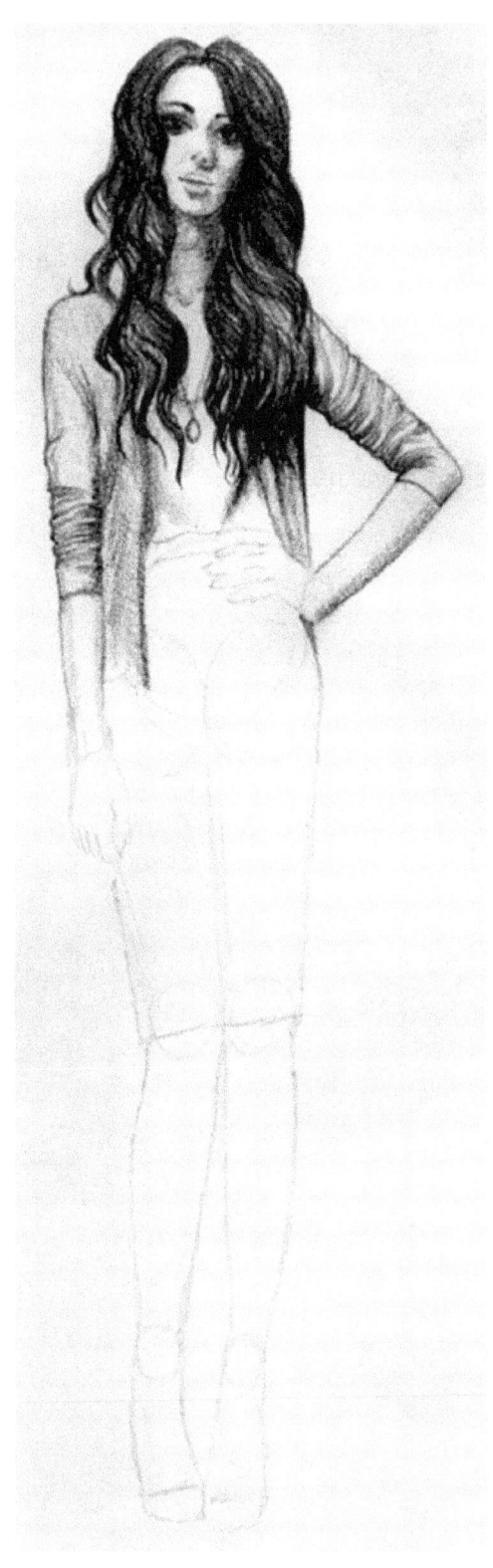

Step 5

Draw the skirt falling till the knees of the lady. Draw a thin belt on the rim of the skirt. Notice the beautiful waves on the skirt arising because of the position of the legs. Give shading in the hands of the girl. Also, draw a broad wristwatch on the left hand of the girl.

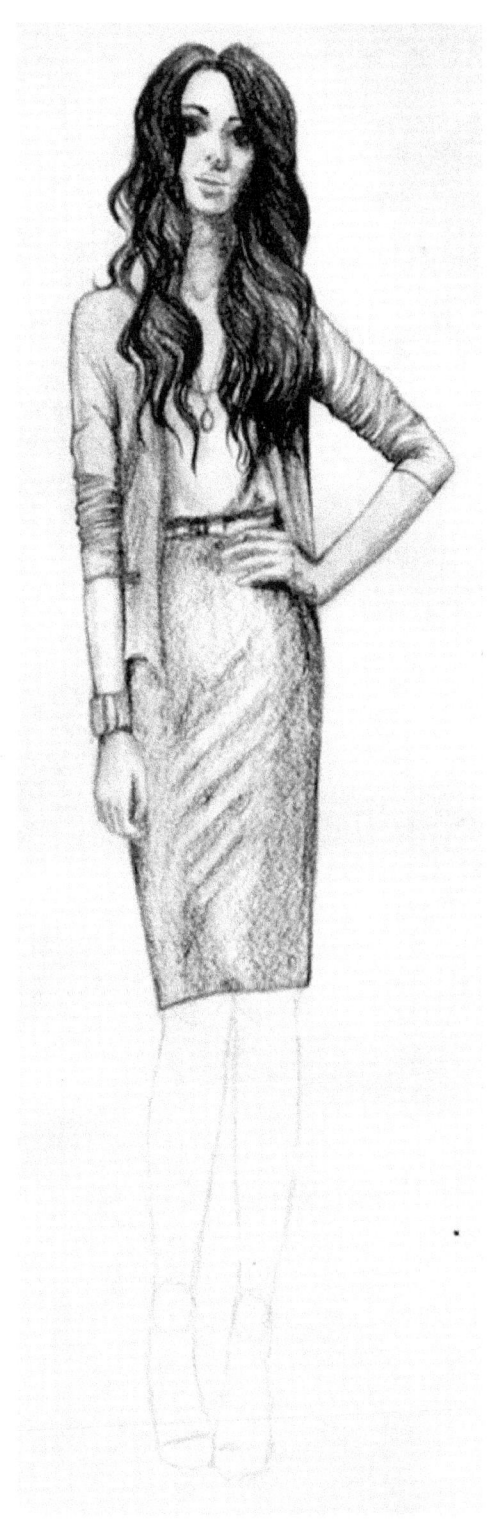

Step 6

Shade the legs of the lady along with her sandals. Since this is the front view of the lady, the heels of the sandals are not visible. But, the position of the feet gives and impression that the lady is wearing heeled footwear.

The lady in formals is complete.

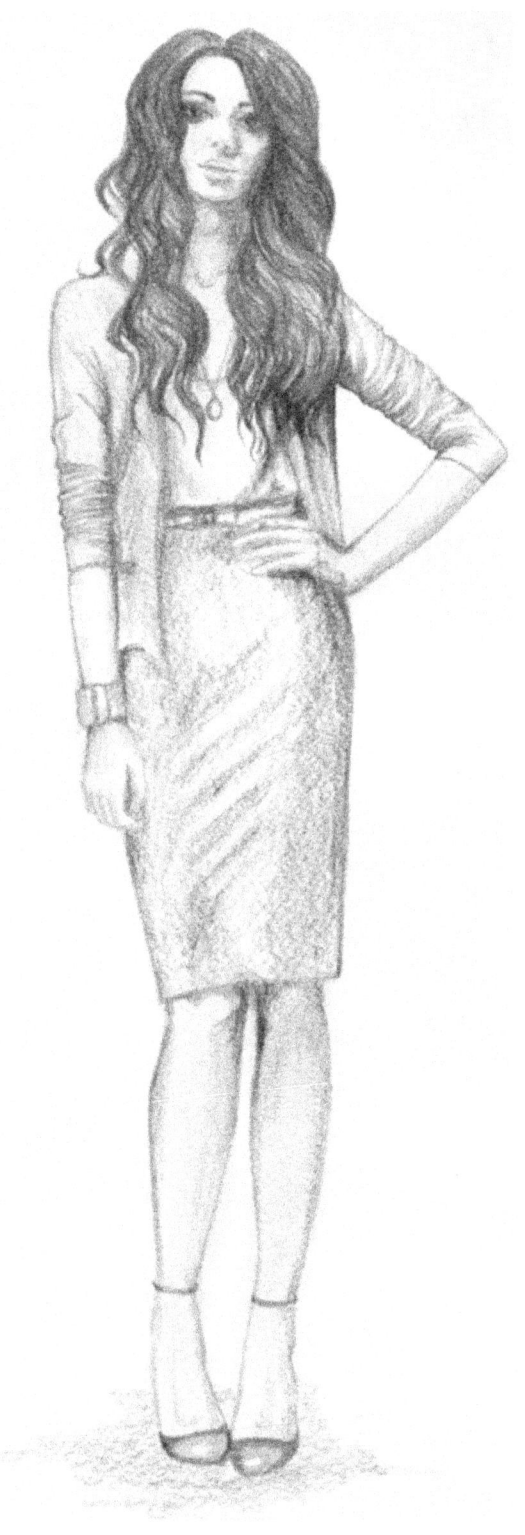

Chapter 6
How to Draw a Man in Formals?

Step 1

After drawing a woman in formals, we will draw a man in formals. This man is shown wearing an elegant suit. He has put one hand on his chin and the other hand is in the pocket of his pants. The face is slightly bent downwards and tilted a little sideways. One of the knees is also bent slightly forward.

Notice the lines running along the length of the pants. They signify the folds of the garment.

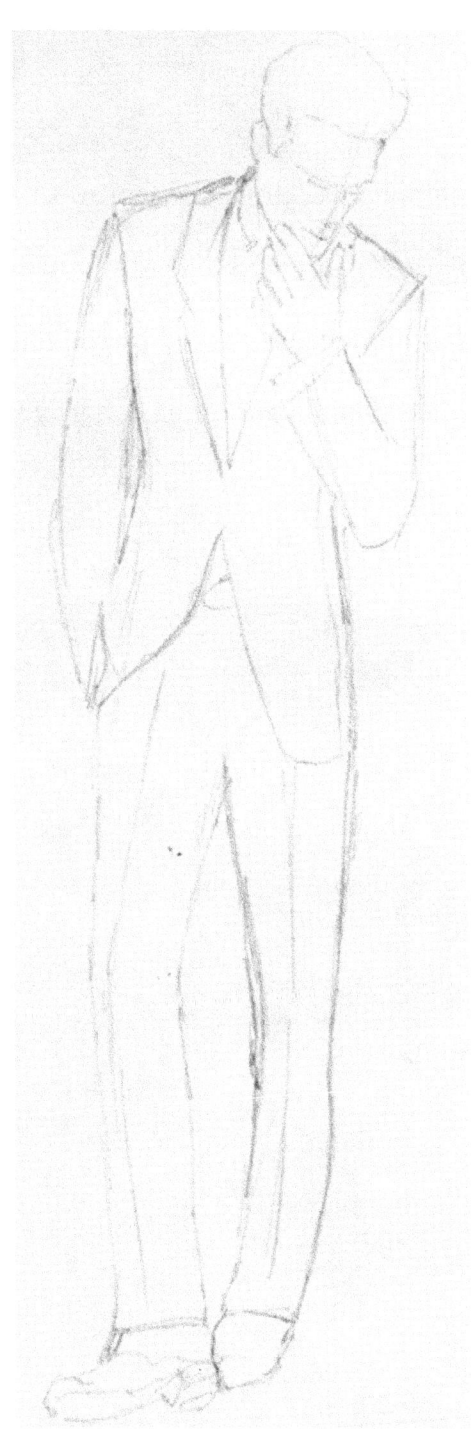

Step 2

Keeping in mind the perspective, draw the features of the face of this man. Since the face is bent downwards, the features are not visible in detail. Moreover, a little area of the face is covered by the hand placed on the chin. Darken the area of the neck visible out of the collar of the shirt.

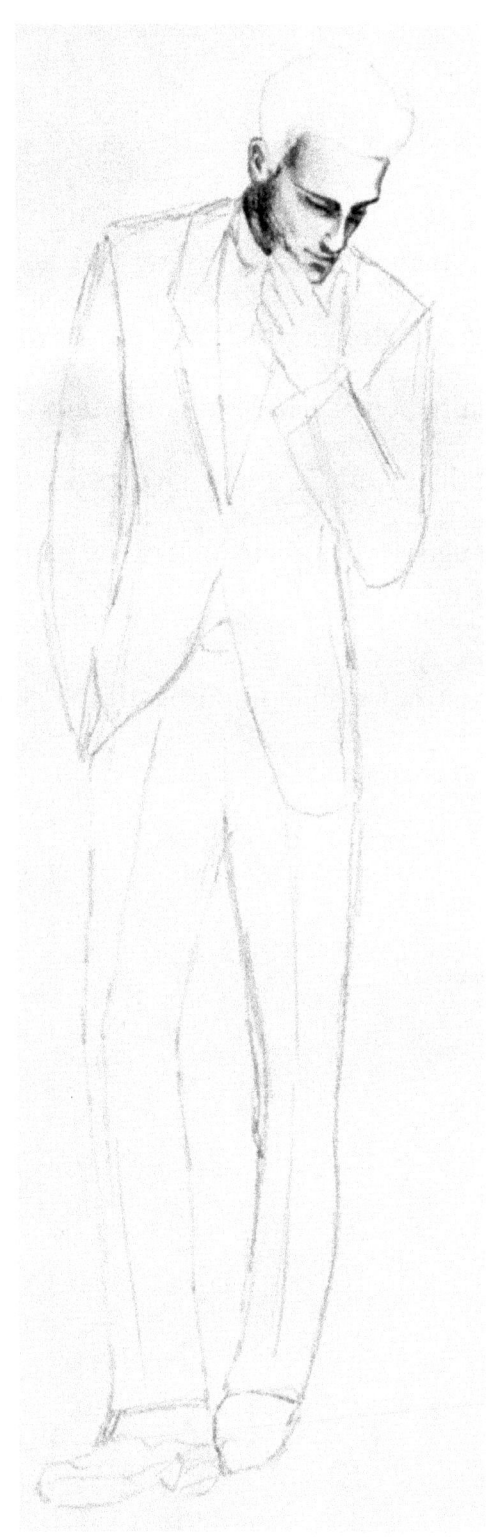

Step 3

Draw the hairs of the man, which are neatly brushed upwards. The front section of the hairs has a shine, which can be shown by leaving the area blank or by using a white pencil. These minor details show that the man is a well-groomed personality. Only a slight change in the quality of hair or anything else may change the complete look of the man.

Give details of the waistcoat visible underneath the coat. The shirt and the tie can also be drawn in this step.

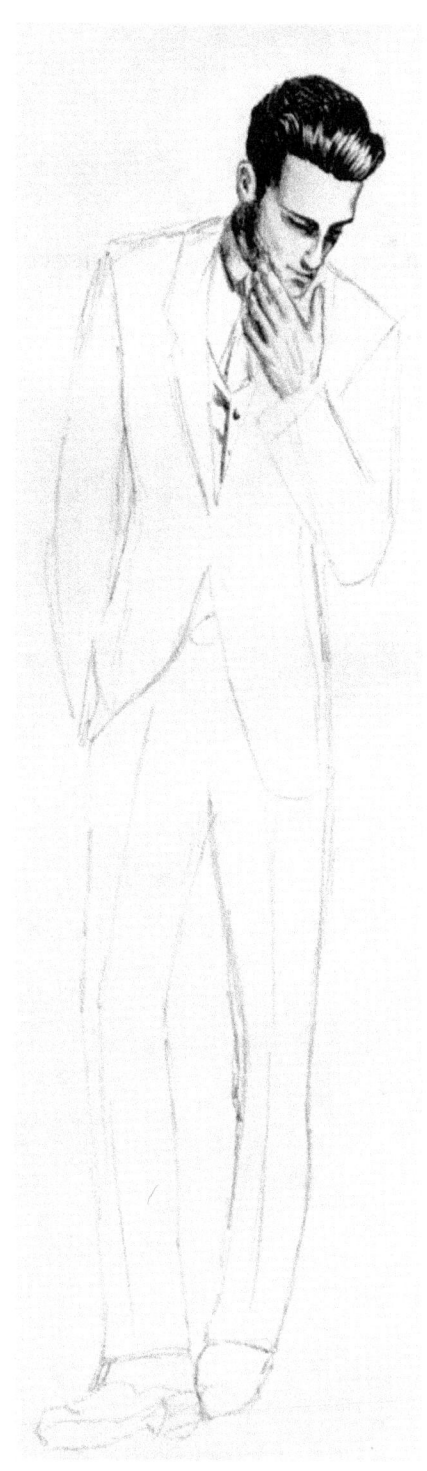

Step 4

Give dark shading in the coat of the man. The sleeve of the shirt on the right hand is also visible coming out of the coat's sleeve. The button of the coat is also given a beautiful shine.

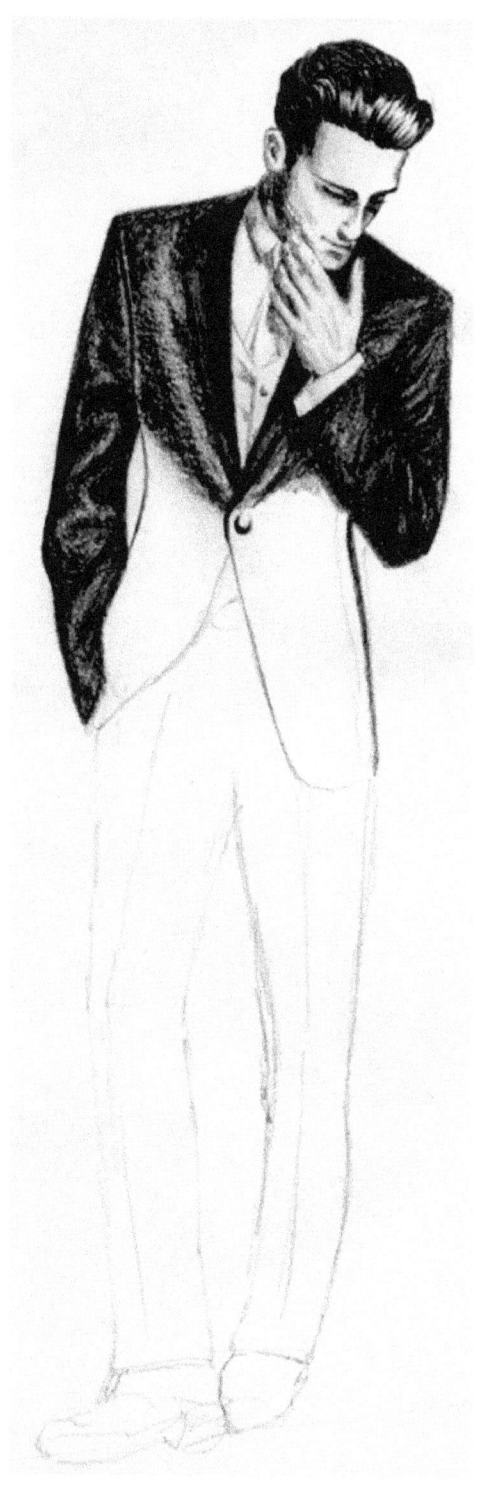

Step 5

Complete the shading in the coat. Give details of the pockets of the coat. Begin shading in the pants specifying its rim and zip. The waves are visible in the pants, which arise out of the position of the legs. The lines we had drawn earlier, running along the length of the pants, are used here to emphasize the folds.

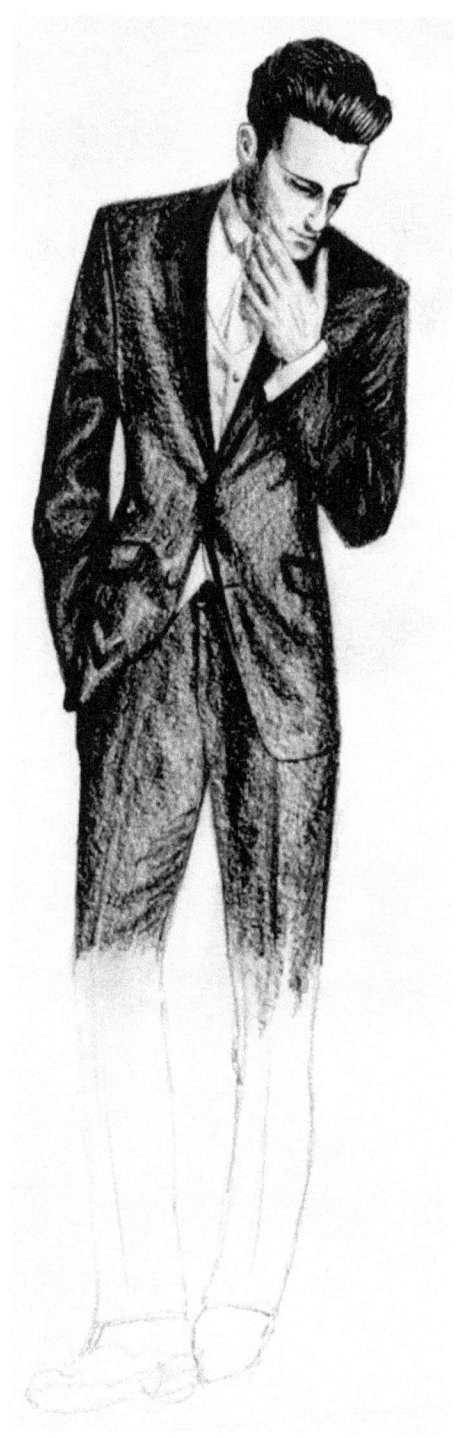

Step 6

Complete the shading in the pants, giving details of the waves in the garment. Draw and shade the formal shoes of the man. The sketch of the man wearing elegant formals is ready.

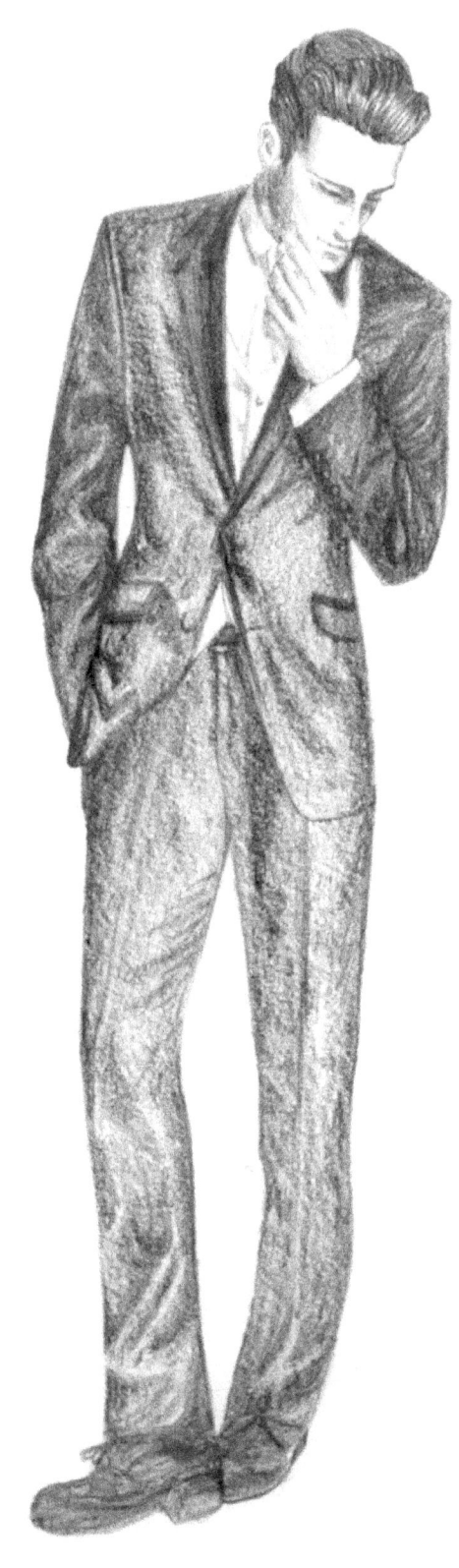

Conclusion

After reading and studying human figures from **How to draw People-Learn How to Draw Women's and Men's Portraits, Human Figures,** you must have got a good idea of drawing human sketches. It is understandable that drawing accurate human figures is not the job of a single day. But, if you practice consistently, you can accomplish your targets in no time.

Like we have said earlier, you have to forget the stigma attached to the drawing of human figures. You just have to draw what your eyes see, not what your "logical" mind tells you to draw. It is easy to draw generic sketches. But, drawing realistic human figures needs detailed observation.

You can begin by drawing human portraits from the photographs of any celebrities, family members, friends or even cartoons. Once you get the hang of drawing human sketches from pictures, you can move ahead to draw live portraits. Ask a friend to pose for you patiently and just grab a pencil to draw the portrait.

Picking up heavier tasks in art is just a matter of taking initiative. Once you gather the courage of foregoing your fears, you can master any form of art. Just proceed and push yourself to draw what you have always wanted. Good luck!

Thank you!

Thank you for choosing our book, we hope you found it interesting and helpful.

If you liked the book, please give us a favor to write your review.

We would really appreciate this!

If you would like to have a bonus – **FREE BOOK**, please send the screenshot of your review to this e-mail:

kelly.artbooks@gmail.com and we will send you a **FREE BOOK** in PDF as a **GIFT!****

Hope to see you in our future books and good luck in your drawing experience!

** in the e-mail subject please mention the name of the book you reviewed and the author.